MW01680168

Martha A. Crawford

DON'T GIVE UP! KEEP GOING!

Fultus™ Books

DON'T GIVE UP! KEEP GOING!

by

Martha A. Crawford

ISBN 1-59682-057-8

Published by Fultus Corporation

Corporate Web Site: http://www.fultus.com
Fultus eLibrary: http://elibrary.fultus.com
Online Book Superstore: http://store.fultus.com
Writer Web Site http://writers.fultus.com/crawford/

To my husband Ray:
Thank you for your support and encouragement.
You are my soul mate and a constant partner in life.
Thank you for letting me be your wife. I love you.

Also, I dedicate this book to the other “joys” in my life:
Dr. Tim, Becky, Mary Kate and Grace Thompson
Clint, Tracy and Laney Crawford
You make my life so much richer. I love you.

Table of Contents

PREFACE

*It is my desire that each of you who reads this devotional book will learn more about our wonderful, marvelous Lord. There are 52 devotions included in **DON'T GIVE UP! KEEP GOING!** Please read the same devotion each day for a week before moving on to the next one. If you will follow the daily instructions below, I feel you will grasp the maximum spiritual thought I pray for you to receive:*

Day 1: Read the complete devotion.

Day 2: Read and study the Scripture references of the devotion from your Bible, including any cross-reference verses and definitions your Bible suggests.

Day 3: Read the complete devotion again.

Day 4: Memorize one of the verses of the reading today.

Day 5: Use today to pray about your spiritual application of what you have learned.

Day 6: Read the complete devotion again.

Day 7: Use the "notes" space at the end of the devotion to write your thoughts, convictions, resolutions, and insights concerning what you have gleaned from the day's reading.

Now, go to the next devotional in the book and follow the same schedule as above.

Thank you for taking the time to read

DON'T GIVE UP! KEEP GOING!

DON'T GIVE UP! KEEP GOING!

"And falling into a place where two seas met, they ran the ship aground; the hinder part was broken with the violence of the waves...they which could swim should cast themselves first into the sea, and get to land; And the rest, some on boards, and some on broken pieces of the ship...that they escaped all safe to land" (Acts 27:41, 43-44, KJV).

"And Noah went in, and his sons, and his wife, and his sons' wives with him, into the ark, because of the waters of the flood" (Genesis 7:7, KJV).

The unvarnished truth is that when life gets in the way, we always have to make adjustments. Often, the unexpected pops its head up at the most inconvenient times. Not always do we know how to cope with these surprises. We tend to be creatures of habit and not like to make necessary adjustments in our daily routines. Sometimes, God allows life to get in the way so we can appreciate the smoother days; the more secure times; the times when we feel safe in our comfort zone. Our son Clint says that the thing that makes the view from a mountaintop look prettier is the valleys one has just traveled.

In Genesis, we read about the flood that caused Noah and his family to change their plans. Not only did they have to get in an ark, they had to build it first. They might have been crowded on the ark. We don't know. The animals probably smelled. Noah and his family might have gotten on each other's nerves. We just don't have a clue to those very personal aspects. They may have wanted to give up and not keep going at times, but they proceeded to do what was necessary.

Acts 27 tells us about how the shipwreck changed the course of action for Paul and the others. They didn't get to shore by boat. When it came apart in the storm, some had to swim and others came in on boards and broken pieces. They didn't give up. They kept going. They reached shore.

Sometimes, the unexpected will happen. Do we want to give up—not go beyond the change? Are we willing to let God make adjustments in our lives?

THOUGHT FOR THE DAY:

Life might get in the way and change my plans, but I will make the necessary adjustments and press on. I can't give up! I won't give up!

PRAYER FOR THE DAY:

Father, help me not begrudge unexpected changes that come my way. Help me to face them. Help me not give up, but to keep going. Father, I know You are there to help me get through the trying times. I can do all things when You are there by my side.

NOTES:

CHOKING IT DOWN!

"If we assay to commune with thee, wilt thou be grieved? but who can withhold himself from speaking" (Job 4:2, KJV)?

"A soft answer turneth away wrath: but grievous words stir up anger" (Proverbs 15:1, KJV).

My father, the late Rev. Ewart Autry, was a country preacher back in the days when churches had no air conditioning. Windows had to be raised to let in a cool breeze. Flies, moths, and other flying organisms would invite themselves to the church services. Once when preaching, a candle fly flew into my father's mouth. It made its way to the back of his throat. He accidentally swallowed and, of course, the little creature went fluttering down. Dad had not planned to have to choke down the candle fly, but circumstances prevailed.

Many times we don't plan to have to choke down unkind words spoken by others, but situations overpower. Eliphaz, Bildad, and Zophar spoke many harsh and damaging words to Job. In Job 3:1, Eliphaz made his first speech, speaking his mind whether Job wanted to hear it or not. It's hard to stay calm when we have to choke down unkind words, but it's important to remember that a soft answer turneth away wrath.

Have I been unkind to someone lately? Have I hurt another by something I said? Have I failed to guard my tongue? Have I forgotten to give a soft answer?

THOUGHT FOR THE DAY:

Today I will think good thoughts and speak kind words. No one will have to grieve because I spoke words that would upset him or her. I will apologize to someone I've hurt in the past with my unguarded tongue.

PRAYER FOR THE DAY:

Father, I pray no one will have to suffer today because I spoke before thinking. Help me to remember that grievous words stir up anger, and that I need to always remember to ask myself what You would say.

NOTES:

WHO, ME! ARE YOU SURE?

"Ye have not chosen me, but I have chosen you..." (John 15:16, KJV).

"And Samuel said unto Jesse, Are here all thy children? And he said, There remaineth yet the youngest, and, behold, he keepeth the sheep...And the Lord said, Arise anoint him: for this is he" (I Samuel 16:11-12, KJV).

We have a neighbor who delights in raising tomatoes. He receives great joy from sharing his bountiful tomato crop with us. Often, he gives green tomatoes as well as ripe ones. We place the green tomatoes on the kitchen windowsill to ripen. A few days later they turn red. It is hard to pick from a row of tomatoes—some large ones—some small ones. However, often I have reached for the most unlikely one—the small one. I know that the small one usually doesn't have a hard center core and is sometimes a sweeter tomato than the most likely big, red, plump one.

In I Samuel, we read about Samuel having Jesse bring all of his sons before him so he could pick a king out of them. When he looked at the row of sons, he asked Jesse if he had any others. Jesse told him he had one more, David, the youngest, a shepherd boy. Samuel told him to send for David. Immediately, when Samuel saw this most unlikely choice from the row of Jesse's sons, he revealed that David was the one the Lord said should be King.

Oh, how unworthy I am to serve the King of Kings and the Lord of Lords. What could He possibly see that would make Him want to use me?

THOUGHT FOR THE DAY:

The most unlikely ones are often the servants God picks to do His great work on earth.

PRAYER FOR THE DAY:

Lord, I am so unworthy to be Your servant. I am the most unlikely of Your children to be about doing Your work. But, Father, if You see anything in me that You can use, I am willing. Here am I, Lord.

NOTES:

I JUST DARE YOU TO...

"And the Philistine said unto David, Am I a dog that thou comest to me with staves? And the Philistine cursed David by his gods. And the Philistine said to David, Come to me, and I will give thy flesh unto the fowls of the air, and to the beasts of the field" (I Samuel 17:43-44, KJV).

"Then said David to the Philistine, Thou comest to me with a sword, and with a spear, and with a shield: but I come to thee in the name of the Lord of hosts..." (I Samuel 17:45, KJV).

"I double-dog dare you," yelled the barefooted boy to his playmate. His big toe drew a line in the dirt to mark off territory not to be crossed.

"I'll come over that line if I want to...you won't stop me," the other boy screamed.

"If you do, you'll wish you hadn't." The confrontation got more intense. The battle was on...

Well, the Bible tells about an entirely different kind of confrontation. It presents one between David and Goliath. Goliath noticed David was coming toward him with a stick and he asked him if he thought he was a dog. David knew he had to hold his ground with this giant. Goliath told David to come on over to where he was and he would give his flesh to the fowls of the air and to the beasts. David stood strong at the dare. He knew he had someone in his army that no man or beast could conquer. David looked at Goliath and told him that he came to him in the name of the Lord of hosts—that God would deliver him into his hand and he would smite him, cut off his head and give the carcasses to the fowls and beasts.

You know the rest of the story. This young man David stood firm so all the earth would know that there was a God in Israel. Goliath went down, defeated, and died.

When faced with giants in our lives, how many times have we run rather than proclaimed God as our Almighty Helper? When have we compromised our beliefs so we could get out of an uncomfortable confrontation with someone? Do we believe God can conquer the giants in our lives? Have we given our Lord a chance to fight our battles?

THOUGHT FOR THE DAY:

What contentment and peace could be in our lives if only we let God fight our giants for us!

PRAYER FOR THE DAY:

Father, I am so tired and weary of having to deal with obstacles that keep me from being what You want me to be. I've tried to fight these giants on my own strength, and I have failed. Please, help me. Take over my battles for me from this day forward. I give them to You, Lord.

NOTES:

JUST WHERE HAVE YOU BEEN, CHILD?

"And when they saw him, they were amazed: and his mother said unto him, Son, why hast thou thus dealt with us? Behold, thy father and I have sought thee sorrowing" (Luke 2:48, KJV).

"For whom the Lord loveth he chasteneth, and scourgeth every son whom he receiveth. If ye endure chastening, God dealeth with you as with sons; for what son is he whom the father chasteneth not" (Hebrews 12:6-7, KJV)?

"You know better than to do that," my dad scolded. My head bowed, tears trickled down my face. I was guilty. Our family outing was wrecked with worry because I wandered into the woods without letting my parents know I was going on a little adventure. What a "stir" I caused!

The Bible tells us that Mary and Joseph went to Jerusalem for the feast of the Passover. When returning home, they discovered Jesus was not with them. They thought he might be with other family members on the journey. He was not there. They sorrowed for their child. Mary and Joseph turned back to Jerusalem. After three days of torture, frantically trying to find their son, they found him in the temple talking and listening to men of knowledge. Mary chastised Jesus because she loved Him. She asked Him why He had dealt with them this way. She said, "...thy father and I have sought thee sorrowing."

Our Heavenly Father has sorrowed after us many times because we have wandered away from Him. He never left us—we did the roaming. God has to chastise us because He loves us. He wants what is good for us. HE WANTS US WITH HIM! Why can't we comprehend that He desires and longs for us to have a daily walk with Him? He doesn't want us to be away from Him--He misses us!

THOUGHT FOR THE DAY:

Today is the appointed time when I will get back close to God. I will not go away from Him again. Nothing will come between my Savior and me.

PRAYER FOR THE DAY:

Master, I come to You with bowed head and broken heart because I have disappointed You. Many times I have strayed away from Your will. I thank You for not giving up on me as I found my journey back to You. Hallelujah to the Lamb.

NOTES:

AMERICA PUT ON YOUR BLUSH!

"Now when Daniel knew that the writing was signed, he went into his house; and his windows being open in his chamber toward Jerusalem, he kneeled upon his knees three times a day, and prayed, and gave thanks before his God, as he did aforetime" (Daniel 6:10, KJV).

"Were they ashamed when they had committed abomination? nay, they were not at all ashamed, neither could they blush: therefore they shall fall among them that fall: at the time that I visit them they shall be cast down, saith the Lord" (Jeremiah 6:15, KJV).

When in elementary school in Hickory Flat, Mississippi, the first thing my class would do each morning was to have a reading from the Bible, say a prayer, and give the Pledge of Allegiance to the United States Flag. These actions were pure, genuine, and wholesome. They served as cornerstones for our lives. There was no way we would be punished for these daily enrichments. Today, students often are not given the privilege to take part in these wonderful building blocks of life.

The Persians made Darius, a Mede, king in Babylon. Daniel was made one of three presidents for the land. The other two presidents didn't like Daniel, so they plotted against him. They knew Daniel prayed to God three times each day, so they met with Darius and asked him to declare a law that no one could pray to anyone but him. If one prayed to someone besides Darius, the person would be thrown to the lions. Daniel continued to pray to God three times each day. He was thrown in a den of lions for punishment.

On the other hand, in Jeremiah 6:10-21, we find Judah being condemned for not heeding the warnings for having no shame, for being stubborn, for empty worship, and other offenses. Unlike Daniel, Judah's people were guilty of compromising. They weren't bold, and strong, and steadfast like Daniel.

Are we a people who refuse to compromise our beliefs? Do we easily give in when the pressure gets heavy so we won't offend others who don't believe in God? Have we reached a point of no return concerning morals, good citizenship, and belief in our Almighty God? Like Judah, is America showing no shame? Does America not blush anymore?

THOUGHT FOR THE DAY:

I will not compromise any of my beliefs for the sake of rejection by a friend or pressure from another person. I will stand my ground concerning my beliefs in my Heavenly Father. I will show other Americans that I am not ashamed of my Lord or His Gospel.

PRAYER FOR THE DAY:

Father, often I'm guilty of standing in the shadow and not SHOWING others that I do have a Master who rules and reigns in my life. Forgive me. Help me to never conduct empty worship. May I be steadfast like Daniel in acknowledging You as Lord and Savior. God, may I as an American realize You are the reason our country has prospered. Help all Americans to put You first.

NOTES:

HIS HONORABLE POSITION

"And behold, a woman in the city, which was a sinner, when she knew that Jesus sat at meat in the Pharisee's house, brought an alabaster box of ointment, and stood at his feet behind him weeping, and began to wash his feet with tears, and did wipe them with the hairs of her head, and kissed his feet, and anointed them with the ointment" (Luke 7: 37-38, KJV).

"And he died in a good old age, full of days, riches, and honour…" (I Chronicles 29:28, KJV).

Cars dashed to the side of the road and stopped. One driver removed his cap and placed it over his heart. Another turned his automobile lights on. The hearse carrying my father's body slowly passed the folk sitting still in their vehicles paying honor to the dead. Being reared in a small Southern town, the tradition of stopping one's automobile as a funeral procession passed was not a surprise to our family. Showing respect and honor to someone who dies exemplifies the fact that the person was loved and will be missed. I once heard a minister say that we should live our lives in such a way that even the undertaker would be sorry we died. He was telling us to live a clean, decent, honest, and honorable life that will set a good example while we are LIVING.

Speaking of honor and respect, our Lord and Savior, Jesus Christ, is worthy of all our praise, honor, glory, respect, and love we can give Him. Luke 7:37-38 tells of a woman in a city, who was a sinner. When she heard Jesus would be at Simon's house, she brought an alabaster box of ointment. This was a long-necked flask which contained fine translucent material used for storing perfume. The woman began washing Jesus' feet with tears, wiping His feet with her hair, kissing them, and anointing them with fine ointment. Simon questioned this sinful woman doing this act. Jesus reprimanded Simon. He said, "Seest thou this woman? I entered into thine house, thou gavest me no water for my feet: but she hath washed my feet with tears, and wiped them with the hairs of her head. Thou gavest me no kiss: but this woman since the time I came in hath not ceased to kiss my feet. My head with oil thou didst not anoint: but this woman hath anointed my feet with ointment" (Luke 7: 44-46, KJV).

THOUGHT FOR THE DAY:

Today, I will honor my Lord and Savior with my prayers. I will tell Him what He means to me. He is King of Kings and Lord of Lords, WORTHY TO BE PRAISED.

PRAYER FOR THE DAY:

Precious Savior, forgive me for forgetting to tell You how much You are worthy of honor. I fail to thank You for loving me. Forgive me when I don't show You the love You so richly deserve. Oh, Holy Master, You are the worthy Lamb.

NOTES:

THE OLD PATHS

"If my people, which are called by my name, shall humble themselves, and pray, and seek my face, and turn from their wicked ways; then will I hear from heaven, and will forgive their sin, and will heal their land" (II Chronicles 7:14, KJV).

"Thus saith the Lord, Stand ye in the ways, and see, and ask for the old paths, where is the good way, and walk therein, and ye shall find rest for your souls. But they said, We will not walk therein" (Jeremiah 6:16, KJV).

Ray and I went walking on our place not long ago. When we go into the woods we see many different kinds of animals. It is so exciting to watch how they maneuver around in their environment. Some run through the forest. Others hop over things. And, then some of these creatures like to crawl. Whichever movement befits them, they leave a path. It may be a path through the grass. It might be a path through the leaves. Some of the animals even leave paths through the mud. Whichever type path is left, other animals can follow. A particular path we noticed was one left by deer. It was easy to tell this path was made the year before. It was an old path, yet, still a good one to follow.

In II Chronicles, God speaks to Solomon. Verse 14 of this chapter is a well-known verse stating God's requirements for blessing: prayer, devotion, humility, and repentance. He's reminding Solomon that his people must go another way from what they've been traveling in their lives. Then, in Jeremiah 6:16, we find that the Lord tells the children of Israel to turn to what is good, right, and lasting, reminding them to "...ask for the old paths, where is the good way, and walk therein."

There are many people I remember who set a wonderfully strong path for me to follow in my growing-up years. They had special ways of doing things that set a good example for me. Oh, how I long to follow the good paths those older people made. Those people and their paths were genuine, pure, and Godly.

GLANCE OVER MY SHOULDER

I hear the quietness in the air and long for a "Hey, how ya'll today?"
Wishing time could be turned back and a friend was a real friend;
A family was still a sacred thing.

I hear the quietness in the air and long for the moment
When "suppertime" was the happy climax to a long day,
And story reading at night was a treat for the young AND the old.

I hear the quietness in the air and long for the time
When family devotion was sweet and sacred for all the members,
And a "good ole talk with the Lord" was "getting a burden-off-your-chest time."

I hear the quietness in the air and long for the time
When all the kids came home for Sunday dinner,
And "washer pitching" under the old oak tree was a Sunday afternoon treat!

I hear the quietness in the air and long to see the family
Goin' together to hear the pastor preach about the coming of the Lord,
And hear the church folk singing *Amazing Grace, When the Roll is Called Up Yonder, and I'll Fly Away.*

I hear the quietness in the air and long for the old-timey revival meetings
That brought out overall-clad farmers who sat outside on their car hoods listening to the old-timey
Preaching through the raised windows of the church house; spitting tobacco on the ground and hollering "AMEN" all in the same breath.

I hear the quietness in the air and long to see babies spread out on pallets on the church floor,
And mothers trying not to disturb the preacher as they unscrewed Mason jar lids to give
Their young'uns a drink of water.

I hear the quietness in the air and long for the wholesome things of life--
Dinner on the grounds, family picnics, sitting in the front porch swing, checker games,
Stringing popcorn for the cedar Christmas tree, baptizing in the river, fried peach pies, bread pudding, milk gravy and homemade biscuits.

Ah, I hear the quietness in the air and I long—long for the old-timey PEACE of days gone by.

By Martha A. Crawford

****

THOUGHT FOR THE DAY:

I will strive to follow the good examples—the old paths—set before me. These old paths and examples are what made homes strong in past years. I will try to make a good path for my family to follow today.

PRAYER FOR THE DAY:

Father, forgive me when I have strayed out of the great and wonderful path You set for me to follow. Please help me today to stay in the middle of the "old paths" of good, Godly ways so that my life will be more like You would have it to be today.

NOTES:

THE CRITICAL ISSUE

"And Miriam and Aaron spake against Moses because of the Ethiopian woman whom he had married: for he had married an Ethiopian woman" (Numbers 12:1, KJV).

"Judge not, and ye shall not be judged: condemn not, and ye shall not be condemned…" (Luke 6: 37, KJV).

Criticism is a very hard thing to take. It can be devastating to the person who has done no wrong, yet is being judged and criticized. We are to love each other—not criticize and judge one another. Miriam and Aaron criticized Moses for marrying an Ethiopian woman. Did they really care who he married? Probably not. The critical underlying issue was their jealously toward Moses because of his high profile and power. They diverted from the real issue and let their feelings splinter out into the form of criticism. They had too much pride to admit their jealously. They put up a smoke screen by attacking Moses' character and his choice of a wife.

The Bible plainly reminds us that we are not to judge each other. However, there is a growing form of criticism that seems to overpower the best of characters. The fact is that critics will be criticized sooner or later. That is when the criticizer has to take some of his or her own medicine. We need to guard against saying unnecessary things about others. It would not be a very pleasant moment to have to face the person we had talked about, and try to explain to them why we had said what we did about them. The best way to avoid a scenario of this sort is to ask ourselves if what we say about someone will make the world a more informed world of truth; a better place. If the answer is no, then stay quiet.

THOUGHT FOR THE DAY:

Criticism of someone is unnecessary and very painful to the person being criticized. I must face the fact that I am far from being perfect and I am in no position to say anything critical about anyone. I was not put here on earth to make others holy. I can't even keep myself holy!

PRAYER FOR THE DAY:

Father, I pray that you will help me not to say anything to, or about, someone in a critical way. Help me to remember that I could be the one being criticized, and I would not enjoy being confronted in that way. If I can't think of anything good to say about my fellowman, then help me to resist the temptation of saying something that might not even be the truth.

NOTES:

IT GOES AND COMES BACK...

"The wind goeth toward the south, and turneth about unto the north; it whirleth about continually, and the wind returneth again according to his circuits" (Ecclesiastes 1:6, KJV).

"For as the rain cometh down, and the snow from heaven, and returneth not thither, but watereth the earth, and maketh it bring forth and bud, that it may give seed to the sower, and bread to the eater" (Isaiah 55:10, KJV).

My nephew, Ronald Autry, is a very special person because he has a wonderful smile, beautiful eyes, contagious personality, and has autism. He spreads joy and love to us, and we love him back. The love goes around. A bad day can be turned into a great one when Ronald walks into one's presence. Often he enthusiastically tells family members about something he saw or heard. Immediately he will say, "And I was so happy!" Ronald spreads happiness and cheer to our lives, and we try to return those things to him.

Ronald has accomplished much in his few years. He not only mastered the difficulties of playing an instrument in his high school band, he was a member of the track team, also. He received an academic award in his high school, and is now a college student. He encouraged his fellow students, as well as his teachers, to do their best. He sent his encouragement around and he saw it coming back to him from everyone with whom he came in contact. Ronald's achievements have been many, even though his autism has made the road more challenging and difficult. But, his parents, Jim Autry and Sally Pederson, would not let him quit or give up. They were, and are, the catalyst in his life. Now all their hard work with him is coming back around to them in the form of seeing their adult son accomplish much more than they ever dreamed. They get to reap the benefits of having a son who brings them many proud moments. They watered and sowed in Ronald's life, and now they are enjoying the beautiful bud.

Our Christian lives should exemplify a spiritual cycle of caring, loving, praying for our fellowman, and witnessing to the lost. These efforts will not come back to us void. The results will go around.

THOUGHT FOR THE DAY:

God's water cycle continuously occurs; water evaporates from the lakes, streams, rivers and sea. It settles on dust particles in the air, condenses and returns to the earth in the form of rain, sleet or snow. Plants grow healthier because of this needed moisture. Like His water cycle, I will send around love, joy and patience to someone's life today, and pray they will use these to nourish someone else's world.

PRAYER FOR TODAY:

Precious Lord, You've shown me love, concern, and encouragement. I pray I will know how to spread these gifts around to someone when they need a friend. You gave to me. Now, please help me give to others.

NOTES:

CARMEN, THE ENCOURAGER

"But none of these things move me, neither count I my life dear unto myself, so that I might finish my course with joy, and the ministry, which I have received of the Lord Jesus, to testify the gospel of the grace of God" (Acts 20:24, KJV).

"That I may come unto you with joy by the will of God, and may with you be refreshed" (Romans 15:3, KJV).

Tears of joy flow from those listening to Carmen Greathouse sing about having a great life. You see, Carmen is a special needs young lady, but she is eager to sing praises of the great life God has given her. Although mentally challenged, she is one of the most creative persons I have ever known. She can hear a song and then sing it, or see examples of arts or crafts and make them. Carmen has a special talent for soothing the hurts of others. She smiles, laughs, cares, cheers the lonely, brings joy to the sad, and spreads God's love everywhere she goes. Carmen "writes" in her own unique way words to tell others how much they are loved by her. She will always remind others that she is praying for them. Her parents Bro. Jimmy Greathouse and his wife Janice have many folk to tell them what a blessing Carmen's little notes are to them. Often Bro. Jimmy and Janice don't even know she's written someone until they are told later. Their hearts swell with joy when they learn of their daughter's ministry of encouragement to others. This special young lady has her own little way of ministering to others in need. I am always refreshed in Carmen Greathouse's presence.

How often do we overlook a chance to help someone else have a great life? "That I may come unto you with joy by the will of God, and may with you be refreshed" (Romans 15:3, KJV).

THOUGHT FOR THE DAY:

I will not pass up a chance to count it a blessing to get to spread joy to someone's life today. I will remind them of the great life we all have simply because God cares for us.

PRAYER FOR THE DAY:

God, forgive me for not emphasizing the good life YOU have given me. Father, help me to spread joy to another person who is having a hard time. With Your help, may I bring cheer and laughter to others.

NOTES:

DADDY, I'M SORRY

"I acknowledged my sin unto thee, and mine iniquity have I not hid. I said, I will confess my transgressions unto the Lord; and thou forgavest the iniquity of my sin. Selah" (Psalm 32:5, KJV).

"Therefore if thou bring thy gift to the altar, and there rememberest that thy brother hath ought against thee; Leave there thy gift before the altar, and go thy way; first be reconciled to thy brother, and then come and offer thy gift" (Matthew 5: 23-24, KJV).

Dear Daddy,

I'm sorry but I did something tonight that I didn't mean to do. It was an accident. I broke your shaving mug. Momma tried to glue it back but it was too broken. I will use my allowance to buy you another one when I can go somewhere to get it. I am very sorry. Please don't be mad at me. I love you, Daddy.

Love,
Clint

Our son Clint was only a young fellow when he wrote this note. Clint knew his loving dad would be faithful to forgive and show him mercy and love. However, he felt the need to confess his mistake and make things right between them.

Our Heavenly Father is faithful to forgive us, but He wants us to forgive others their trespasses, also. On the other end of the spectrum we want mercy, grace, and forgiveness, but find it difficult to give our apology to someone else. Christ set a wonderful example for us when he went among those who hated him. He showed compassion and forgiveness. Why do we sometimes find it so hard to forgive? Why do we often have to make ourselves apologize so we can receive forgiveness? Oh, that we might be more like Jesus in this area of our lives.

Psalm 32 is an account of how merciful and forgiving God was to David. The first verse of Psalm 32 says, "Blessed is he whose transgression is forgiven, whose sin is covered."

THOUGHT FOR THE DAY:

I will have a heart of forgiveness toward my fellowman today. If I wrong someone today, I will apologize and ask for their forgiveness. May I be reminded to offer grace and mercy to others.

PRAYER FOR THE DAY:

Father, sometimes it is difficult to forgive others. I can't conquer this sin without Your help. I know I must forgive in order to be forgiven by You, Lord. So, I am asking You to replace resentment in my life with Your peace, love, and forgiveness.

NOTES:

IT'S CLUCKING TIME!

"...how often would I have gathered thy children together, even as a hen gathereth her chickens under her wings..." (Matthew 23: 37, KJV).

"...hide me under the shadow of they wings" (Psalm 17:8, KJV).

A great learning experience in my life was 4-H Club. It was the foundation for many things that I do today. We learned to cook, sew, judge different foods and crops, make public speeches, and many other quality skills. One of my favorite learning experiences was raising Rhode Island Red Chickens. There is much to be said about the chicken family. They are a close knit bunch. Mother hens patiently wait until their baby chicks peck through the egg shell. As soon as their wobbly little legs can maneuver, they begin to follow their mother. She takes them on a great expedition of finding food. Once a worm or a bug has been sited in the ground, the hen demonstrates how to capture it. The mother hen clucks when she wants her babies to follow along behind her. All is well until a threat of danger surfaces. Immediately, she raises her wings, sends out a special cluck alarm, and the chicks race under her wings. The mother hen shields her offspring of impending harm.

Our granddaughters, Mary Kate and Grace, daughters of Dr. Tim and Becky Thompson, have been brought up in a loving protective home. When younger, Mary Kate and Grace would hide behind their mom's skirt or climb up in their dad's lap when someone unfamiliar would come into their territory. They knew they were safe as long as mom and dad were near. As soon as Tim or Becky put their arms around them, everything in their world was made secure.

Our Lord, the great Protector, takes care of us in danger. He is there for us to run under His wings of safety and love. He calls out to us. It's in our best interest to quickly go to Him. Then, and only then, will everything be all right in our world.

THOUGHT FOR THE DAY:

No one loves me like Jesus. When I feel lonely, He hugs me. When I am afraid, He's my great Protector. He hears my cry and quickly hovers over me.

PRAYER FOR THE DAY:

Father, I thank You for the times when You protected me when I couldn't protect myself. I was safe under Your wings. Help me to remember You are always near; ready to take care of my every need. Please help me to listen when YOU CALL.

NOTES:

ABUSED

"And they stoned Stephen, calling upon God, and saying, Lord Jesus, receive my spirit" (ACTS 7:59, KJV).

"And she came in straightway with haste unto the king, and asked, saying I will that thou give me by and by in a charger the head of John the Baptist" (Mark 6:25, KJV).

There are many persons in this world who are battered and bruised. Abuse is at its highest level. My poem, *Battered and Bruised,* exemplifies the frightening fact that so many innocent victims have gone through abuse, yet, had no one they felt they could talk to who would believe them.

BATTERED AND BRUISED

Don't hit me! Please, don't hit me again.
I crawled from the floor onto the sofa –
Knots and bruised skin; pain running down my body;
My heart beating so fast I thought my life would end.

My very soul in despair; heart and mind numb from pain and fear-
Lying coldly still to ward off another slap, more pain;
Wishing life would free me from this monster I once
Loved more than life itself.

Hours of therapy would never have erased the death
Wish in his eyes for me during his madness; a
Death wish I knew could come true anytime, any
Day; a wish that only I could recognize during these

Frequently dreaded "spells" abruptly appearing in his head.

All the "I'm sorry, I won't do it again" sentences were only cover-ups
For the next time of outraged anger; times of loaded guns held to my head,
Promising me no future at all if I did not stop crying and begging for mercy – just mercy.

Each day brought a new challenge – one of gambling on the right
Words to say, the right things to do. Never knowing what "material"
Bribe would be offered me in exchange for silence to the family on the subject.

Survival techniques became the entertainment of my mind: my escape,
My peace, my safety became obsessions night and day. I prayed that
Sunshine, a drop of dew, a rainbow would all become alive again in my life.

Heart broken, body weakened, spirit battered and bruised – my crushed
Self-esteem left me longing to tell someone, anyone. But, I knew that
After years of silence no one, no one, would believe me.

By Martha A. Crawford

****

The Bible tells us about Stephen being stoned. There is an account of John the Baptist being beheaded. In the twenty-seventh chapter of Matthew, we read about our Lord and Savior being abused by the chief priests and elders. They placed a crown of thorns on His head, spit upon Him, smote Him, mocked Him, and led the Lamb away to be crucified.

THOUGHT FOR THE DAY:

Have I abused and taken advantage of Christ today? Did I abuse Him with my mouth, my thoughts, and my heart? I will be mindful of those around me and will earnestly commit to not crucifying anyone with my mouth, thoughts, or heart.

PRAYER FOR THE DAY:

Savior, thank You for dying a cruel death on the cross so that sinners such as I could be saved. Help me to always be mindful of how You suffered for me.

Father, may I always be a good listener to those abused souls around me so that they will know I really care about them.

NOTES:

JESUS

THE

INNOCENT

SWEET--------LAMB--------OF GOD

PAID

IT

ALL

FOR

SINNERS

"CAW" TO THE END

"And now, Lord, what wait I for? My hope is in thee" (Psalm 39:7, KJV).

"...for he hath said, I will never leave thee, nor forsake thee" (Hebrews 13:5b, KJV).

My husband Ray had a pet crow when he was young. Joe the crow waited anxiously for him to come out of the house each morning. The bird flew excitedly as soon as it saw Ray or heard his voice. Then Ray walked one-fourth of a mile to school with Joe perched on his shoulder. From 8 a.m. to 3 p.m. each day the crow waited for Ray in a tree or on the windowsill outside the classroom. At the end of the day of classes, they made their journey home. The black crow was faithful, never compromising his dedication to his owner.

One Thursday afternoon the bell rang promptly at 3 p.m. Ray approached the outside where he usually met Joe each afternoon. The shiny, black crow lay lifeless on the windowsill. A classmate had killed Joe with his slingshot just before Ray arrived. The pet was faithful to his friend to the end.

The Lord shows us in Hebrews 13:5 that He will be faithful and never leave or forsake us. In Psalm 39:7 we read that David acknowledges that his hope is in Christ. Are we willing to be faithful to God until our death? Do we love Him that much?

The crow's faithfulness to its owner spoke volumes. It had no idea of the fate that lay ahead that day. If Jim could have spoken, I'm sure he would say, "My friend, I didn't plan to leave you or forsake you. I wanted to 'caw' for you until the end. "

Praise be to God, we have the comfort that our Heavenly Father will always be with us no matter what comes our way. He will be our great comforter, our protector, our companion, our strength. He will lead us through the valleys and point us toward the mountains. We don't have to dread or fear we will not be with Him if we have accepted Him as our Lord and Savior.

THOUGHT FOR THE DAY:

Inconsistent faithfulness to the Lord will cripple one's walk with Him. Today, He will find me faithful until the end.

PRAYER FOR THE DAY:

Lord, I'm sorry You have not always found me faithful to You and Your work. Forgive me when I don't show my appreciation that Thy Son was faithful to die on the cross so that sinners such as I could be saved. Thank You for giving me another chance to prove my love for Thee.

NOTES

WHO IS THAT BEHIND THE SCENES?

"Take heed that ye do not your alms before men, to be seen of them: otherwise ye have no reward of your Father which is in heaven" (Matthew 6:1, KJV).

"That thine alms may be in secret: and thy Father which seeth in secret himself shall reward thee openly" (Matthew 6:4, KJV).

Mrs. Debbie Ragland, wife of evangelist, Bro. Mike Ragland, of Hayden, Alabama spends an enormous amount of time supporting her husband in the ministry of carrying God's word. One of the great ministries in their lives is Living Waters Youth Camp. Children and youth from far and near come to the camp each summer to learn more about Jesus. Many young souls have been saved there.

There is much "behind the scenes" work to do at Living Waters Youth Camp. "Miss Debbie," as she is lovingly called by most, does many of the things about which no one knows. She cooks the meals each day for all of the youth and staff at the camp, makes bookmarks, designs Bible verse cards, publishes cookbooks, fervently prays and studies the Word, irons Bro. Mike's white shirts, does the bookkeeping and correspondence, counsels, and takes care of many other things. She is a wife, mother, mother-in-law, grandmother, and a hard worker at anything she attempts. If she isn't doing the above work, she is organizing her ladies' meeting that she has at the camp, or is preparing a talk to present somewhere else to ladies. However, "Miss Debbie" never wants to be noticed or bragged on for anything. She knows what the Lord wills for her to do and it doesn't bother her if she is not the main star. By that I mean she doesn't seek to be THE MAIN STAR. "Miss Debbie" is not a glory-seeker! She willingly gives all the glory, honor, and praise to her Lord. Bro. Mike readily admits he always needs his wife to be his helpmate in his ministry for the Lord. He considers her humbleness to truly be a blessing in his life.

THOUGHT FOR THE DAY:

Today, I will do something special for someone and not let them know who did the deed. I will be honored to give the Lord all the glory He so richly deserves.

PRAYER FOR THE DAY:

Father, forgive us if we seek recognition from man. Help us to always brag on Your greatness and put self aside. Help us never to be "glory" seekers.

NOTES:

GOOD NAME, CHARACTER AND REPUTATION

"A good name is rather to be chosen than great riches, and loving favour rather than silver and gold" (Proverbs 22:1, KJV).

"...give me neither poverty nor riches; feed me with food convenient for me: Lest I be full, and deny thee, and say, Who is the Lord? Or lest I be poor, and steal, and take the name of my God in vain" (Proverbs 30: 8-9, KJV).

When I was young, I would go out with friends. Before leaving, one of my parents would always say, "Just remember who you are." Quite frankly, I never could figure out how they thought I could forget who I was. It was not until later years that I understood what they meant when they said, "Just remember who you are." This statement meant that they wanted me to keep my name and character clean. My mother and dad didn't want me to get careless and blemish my reputation, plus embarrass them. No money or fun is worth one losing his or her good name and character.

Now that I am a mother and grandmother, I completely understand why my mother and dad continuously cautioned me to be on guard against letting the devil lead me off into things that would totally ruin my life and my witness for the Lord.

Nothing is so important that it could replace the good reputation of a person. Have we done something to cause God to be sad? Have we blemished our Christian witness? Does the Lord hang His head in disgust because of the way we have represented ourselves?

Proverbs 22:1 refers to good character and the reputation that should go with it. Proverbs 30: 8-9 deals with Agur praying for these qualities. He asks for circumstances which will not endanger his character. Are we serious enough about keeping a good name, character, and reputation? Do we pray as Agur prayed?

THOUGHT FOR THE DAY:

Is one moment of careless living worth losing a good name, character and reputation?

PRAYER FOR THE DAY:

Lord, help me to stop and think before I do something without asking Your advice and permission. Father, may I never get so careless that my Christian witness doesn't matter to me anymore. Guide me so that I won't become irresponsible.

NOTES:

THE GRAPES OF KNOWLEDGE

"And they came unto the brook of Eshcol, and cut down from thence a branch with one cluster of grapes, and they bare it between two upon a staff..." (Numbers 13:23, KJV).

"And they told him, and said, we came unto the land whither thou sentest us, and surely it floweth with milk and honey; and this is the fruit of it" (Numbers 13:27, KJV).

The Lord spoke to Moses and told him to send his men to search the land of Canaan. Moses sent the spies and told them to find out all they could about the land, people, cities, dwellings, wood, fruits, and other pertinent facts. He told them to be of good courage and bring of the fruit of the land. It was time for the first ripe grapes. After forty days, they returned. It took two of them to bring back just one branch with a cluster of grapes, carrying it on a staff. They gained the knowledge they went after and brought back proof of their journey.

The Holy Bible is full of knowledge that we desperately need to know. If we searched the Scriptures only forty days, we would not come close to finding all the answers to our spiritual questions. Would we be persistent enough to learn what God is trying to show us, and then share the grapes of knowledge with a lost and dying world? James 1:22 states, "But be ye doers of the word, and not hearers only..."

Can the world see the fruit of our gleaning the Scriptures? Oh, that we might be busy sowing to a lost world the Biblical knowledge that we have reaped. We are so often guilty of reaping much more than we ever sow. Who can we share the knowledge of Jesus Christ with today?

THOUGHT FOR THE DAY:

Today I will find a new truth in God's Holy Word. I will share the fruit of my research with someone who doesn't know the Lord as their Savior.

PRAYER FOR THE DAY:

Father, I know it is Your will that I read and learn everything about Your Holy Word. Help me find the time in my busy schedule to search the land of spiritual knowledge in Thy Scriptures. Lord, show me a person in my community who needs to have Your Word shared with them today.

NOTES:

THE "BIGGEST" AND "BESTEST" GIFT

"...Remember the words of the Lord Jesus, how he said, It is more blessed to give than to receive" (Acts 20:35, KJV).

"Every man according as he purposeth in his heart, so let him give; not grudgingly, or of necessity: for God loveth a cheerful giver" (II Corinthians 9:7, KJV).

When my husband Ray was a little boy, he attended a small rural school. Each year at Christmas the students in every class drew names. They brought that person a present to school the last day before classes dismissed for holidays. All of the presents were placed under a huge Christmas tree on the stage in the auditorium. One by one the presents were given to the students. Ray waited anxiously for his name to be called. The last present under the tree was given out. His name was never called. The person drawing his name did not come to school that day and he was heartbroken. Ray pouted all the way home. When he entered the door his mother immediately knew something had gone wrong in her little son's world. She took him in her arms, soothed his pain, and had a talk with him. After hearing Ray's story about not receiving a gift, his mother wisely explained that it is much better to give than to receive. She walked with him to the kitchen, served him a cookie and a glass of milk, and helped the little fellow get over his hurt.

Christ gave us the greatest gift we will ever receive—the gift of dying on the cross so that sinners might be saved. Hallelujah to the Lamb! Hallelujah to the Lamb!

THOUGHT FOR THE DAY:

There is joy in giving to others when one knows the deed may never be returned. As a matter of fact, giving under those circumstances is the ultimate heart of giving.

PRAYER FOR THE DAY:

Savior, help me never to give in expectation of receiving something. Help me to be willing to do a good deed for someone over and over even when they don't say, "Thanks." All that matters is that we give of ourselves and please You. I often forget to stop and thank You for giving Your life on the cross. Please forgive me for not taking the time to dwell upon all You have done for me. You truly are the "biggest" and "bestest" gift of all.

NOTES:

DO YOU SEE WHAT I'M SAYING?

"I have heard of thee by the hearing of the ear: but now mine eye seeth thee" (Job 42:5, KJV).

"Lo, mine eye hath seen all this, mine ear hath heard and understood it" (Job 13:1, KJV).

"Do you "SEE" what I'm "SAYING" is a very common term used in the South. The person is actually asking the listener if he completely understands. To SEE what someone is SAYING is the ultimate acknowledgement of the message being spoken.

"Let me have your eyes—let me have your ears. If I have your eyes, then I have your ears," says Bro. Mike Ragland. Bro. Mike is an Evangelist from Hayden, Alabama and he uses this expression in his sermons when he especially wants the congregation to catch a very specific point he is saying to them. He is letting them know that he desires their full attention. Bro. Mike travels thousands of miles each year preaching the Word that the Lord has put on his heart to say. He desires his listeners to "SEE" what he's "SAYING."

Often, God speaks to us and sends us messages in many ways such as through a picture, a book, a spoken word, a person, or a still small voice. In Job 42:5 no form of God appeared in the whirlwind. But, what God showed about Himself enabled Job to understand. Job listened. Job saw. Job very well knew the significance of the eye-gate and the ear-gate.

If only we could be like Job and let the Lord show us what He wills us to see, and listen to what He wants us to hear. We must not put a "lock" on the eye-gate and ear-gate.

THOUGHT FOR THE DAY:

Just because we "look" doesn't mean we "see." Just because we "hear" doesn't mean we are "listening."

PRAYER FOR THE DAY:

Dear Lord, I want to hear You speak to me so I won't go down the wrong path. Help me to pay close attention to Your instructions so that I will "listen" rather than just hear You. Father, help me to see Your mighty works in my life and know that You will never lead me in the wrong direction.

NOTES:

HIS PRESENCE IS NEAR

"...and, lo, I am with you alway, even unto the end of the world. Amen" (Matthew 28:20, KJV).

"For I am with thee..." (Acts 18:10, KJV).

An elderly lady lives a neighbor to us. Each winter morning one can see smoke coming from the chimney of her tiny frame home. There is wood stacked outside with which to build fires in the fireplace. Her dog lies on the front porch. Birds flock around her bird feeders. However, she is rarely seen. But, one can count on seeing that small whirling gray-white smoke drifting from her chimney, signaling all is well; her presence is nearby. I find a comfort in knowing that our neighbor is functioning in her world even if I don't see her.

God has been near many times when I didn't notice. He has protected me when I couldn't protect myself. My Father has understood me when I couldn't understand my own feelings. He has never forgotten where I was. Sometimes, I have failed to let Him know what comfort He has brought me.

When I was small, I greatly feared storms. My little mind would think that the storm would blow my family members away and we would never see each other again. I would start crying. Often, the electricity would go off and we would be in the dark. At that point I would feel my mom's arms caress me. I couldn't see her in the dark, but I knew she was near. The reassurance of her presence calmed me. I think of how calm I should be in my life knowing that my magnificent Heavenly Father's presence hovers over me. No, I can't see Him, but I know He's there.

THOUGHT FOR THE DAY:

God's presence is all around us—in the breeze, in a bird's song, a baby's smile and a sunset. We don't have to search to find Him—He's there!

PRAYER FOR THE DAY:

Abba, Father, I pray I will always stop and notice that You are near me all the time. Let me remember the words of that great hymn, *What a Friend We Have in Jesus.*

NOTES:

MY NET IS ABOUT TO BURST!

"...go thou to the sea, and cast an hook, and take up the fish that first cometh up; and when thou hast opened his mouth, thou shalt find a piece of money..." (Matthew 17:27, KJV).

"Then Jesus saith unto them, Children, have ye any meat? They answered him, No. And he said unto them, Cast the net on the right side of the ship, and ye shall find. They cast therefore, and now they were not able to draw it for the multitude of fishes" (John 21: 5-6, KJV).

An evangelist preached at our church and used Matthew 17:27 as part of his text. He loves to fish, so he vividly explained this verse. He chuckled after reading Matthew 17:27 and said, "I told you fishing pays off!"

When I was just a little girl, one of the things I loved to do was go fishing. My dad and mother would take my brothers and me to Tippah River close to our home so we could fish for enjoyment AND food. In those days when there wasn't much money, the Lord always provided food in the form of fish. No, we never opened the mouth of a fish and found money. However, the Lord filled our net of need each day. Often, we would fish the biggest portion of the day and it seemed we weren't going to catch even one fish. Then the Lord would come by, and we would have an ample supply of fish for food for the whole next week. And, the Lord didn't even have to throw a line in the water!

We often think God isn't focusing on our needs. But, He will fill the net of needs if only we have faith and do not limit Him to how much we LET Him do.

THOUGHT FOR THE DAY:

God, I need You. Am I limiting You as to how much I allow You to do in my life?

PRAYER FOR THE DAY:

Father, I have let You down many times, but You have never let me down. Help me to remember that You will ALWAYS supply my needs, if only I believe.

NOTES:

"COME ALONG NOW..."

"And the Spirit and the bride say, Come. And let him that heareth say, Come. And let him that is athirst come. And whosoever will, let him take the water of life freely" (Revelation 22:17, KJV).

"My sheep hear my voice, and I know them, and they follow me" (John 10:27, KJV).

In our small town of Blue Mountain, Mississippi there lived a lady doctor. She made house calls, tending the sick and delivering babies. She practiced medicine for many years in two rooms of her home that she had converted into office space. Each year, hundreds of people came to receive the country doctor's help. One patient would leave out of her office and she would come to the waiting room door, point to the next patient and say, "Come along now." The doctor didn't have a nurse or a receptionist to keep up with which patient should be treated next, but she somehow kept up with the information. She never charged the same price from one visit to the next—sometimes not charging at all. The old country lady doctor knew us by name and we knew her familiar voice. We would follow her because we trusted her medical skills.

Jesus says that His sheep know His voice and He knows them. The sheep trust their Savior and follow Him. In Luke 5:27, Levi heard Jesus say, "Follow me," and he left all, rose up, and went with Him. Why can't we trust our Shepherd 100 percent and follow Him? He wants us to "come along."

What a beautiful passage we find in Revelation 22:17. This verse contains four invitations to the unsaved to come to Christ in faith for eternal life. The Spirit it mentions is the Holy Spirit. The bride is the church. The water of life is eternal life. It's available—a free gift—by faith in Christ. All God wants is for us to come to Him.

THOUGHT FOR THE DAY:

From now on, I have decided to follow my Shepherd. I'll be listening for His call. Wherever He wants to lead me, I want to go.

PRAYER FOR THE DAY:

Father, help us to learn Your way and follow when we hear Your voice. Help us to be EAGER and EXCITED about "coming along" with You.

NOTES:

THE LIGHT'S IN MY EYES!

"For with thee is the fountain of life: in they light shall we see light" (Psalm 36:9, KJV).

"...I am the light of the world: he that followeth me shall not walk in darkness, but shall have the light of life" (John 8:12, KJV).

I had this little light in a jar and it was shining. No, it wasn't a light bulb. I had a lightening bug. When we were small, my brothers and I would go outside at night. Sparkling everywhere were these awesome little creatures. Our yard favored a gigantic lighted Christmas tree. We would see how many "little lights" we could catch and put in our jars. We would poke holes in the jar lid so the lightening bugs would be comfortable. After collecting several of these little live blinking creatures, my brothers and I would take them into a dark room in the house to watch them twinkle. A count was taken to see who had the most bugs in their jar.

When I was a small child I loved to sing a song about "this little light of mine." I would sing loudly when I got to the part about "I'm going to let it shine." Today, many souls are groping in darkness, desperately looking for the Light. They haven't figured out that the LIGHT OF THE WORLD is Jesus. He wants to light our paths and He wants His light to shine through our lives.

THOUGHT FOR THE DAY:

Lord, I sometimes block Your light out of my life. My world would not be so dark at times if only I would let You be the LIGHT. Oh, that I can sing the words, "this little light of mine," and then want to let it shine-- let it shine for You, Lord.

PRAYER FOR THE DAY:

Precious Father, please help me to let You shine so that others can see You through my life. Your LIGHT is brighter and greater than any man-made light. Help me not to block Your light out of my needy soul. I want to say, "The **LIGHT'S** in my eyes!"

NOTES:

HIDING OUT

"...he hath hid himself among the stuff" (I Samuel 11:22, KJV).

"Can any hide himself in secret places that I shall not see him..." (Jeremiah 23:24, KJV)?

Hide-and-go-seek has been a favorite game of children for years. One child is the seeker and the rest of the participants hide. Some could find better "stuff" to hide behind than other players. Oh, what fun when someone is finally found in their hiding place! Shouts of, "I found you, I found you," ring out across the yard.

Small animals hide from larger predators. The sun "hides" behind the clouds. The cat hides from the dog. I even saw a child cover his own eyes one time, thinking he was "hidden" and couldn't be seen by anyone. We could go on and list page after page of things that hide.

Have we ever considered the Christian hiding from God? Often, we carelessly think we can hide from God so He won't see us hiding behind the "stuff" of life. There have been many preachers, Sunday School teachers, choir members, nursery workers, unbelievers, and others who have felt the call of God on them, but tried to run and hide. We forget He is all seeing, all hearing, and all knowing. There is no place on the face of this earth that we could hide from God. He can always find us. He wants to talk with us and hold us. God wants us to come out from hiding behind the "stuff" of our lives and spend time with Him. The Lord wants us to stop trying to hide and make excuses for not letting Him have His way with us.

THOUGHT FOR THE DAY:

The best hiding place is in Jesus' arms. In His arms, you'll never WANT to hide or make excuses to Him again.

PRAYER FOR THE DAY:

Heavenly Father, I don't ever want to hide from what You have for me to do here on earth. Help me never to hide behind the "stuff" of life. Help me not find excuses when I don't feel like serving You.

NOTES:

GOING HOME

"Then the disciples went away again unto their own home" (John 20:10, KJV).

"And God shall wipe away all tears from their eyes; and there shall be no more death, neither sorrow, nor crying, neither shall there be any more pain..." (Revelation 21:4, KJV).

Years ago when I started teaching school I was assigned to a first grade reading class. I was trained to be a secondary science teacher, but this was the only job available at the time. This was my first time to teach school and the students' first time to attend class. All of us wanted to cry. There was one particular little fellow who was severely distressed about having to leave his mother and face the real world. He would cry each day until he was exhausted. After a few days into the year, I kept him in at recess so we could have a one-on-one discussion concerning his unhappiness.

"Jacob, can you tell me why you cry all day?" I asked. "Do you feel bad or do you not like school?"

Tears raced down the little fellow's cheeks. Jacob bellowed out, "I just want to go to the house!"

This tiny little student knew that home represented security, love, comfort, hugs, and mother.

Do we long to go to our Heavenly home where we know our Father is waiting with open arms to comfort, love, and welcome us? Our God is at that eternal place where there will be no more tears or sorrow. What a great reunion day that will be!

THOUGHT FOR THE DAY:

Sometimes God washes our eyes with tears so that we can truly see Him and feel His presence in a mighty way.

PRAYER FOR THE DAY:

Precious Lord, I pray I will always allow You to comfort me. Help me to recognize when Your arms are around me—soothing away the hurt. You never said we wouldn't have bad times and shed some tears, but You did promise You would be there to comfort us through those valleys. Thank You for that great assurance, Father.

NOTES:

HONOR AND RESPECT

"There is a generation that curseth their father, and doth not bless their mother" (Proverbs 30:21, KJV).

"Honour thy father and thy mother: that thy days may be long upon the land which the Lord thy God giveth thee" (Exodus 21:5, KJV).

"Yes, Sir" and "No, Sir" were some of the first words I learned to speak. My parents would quickly discipline me if I dare forget to speak in a respectful way to them. Honor for my parents was not an option in life. It was taught to me in such a way that I knew there would be no such thing as breaking the rule without having to suffer the consequence.

Recently, my husband Ray and I were eating in a local restaurant. A young mother and her daughter came in the door arguing because the child refused to put on her shoes. The more the mother yelled at the child, the louder her young daughter screamed in protest. Exhausted, the mother knelt on her knees and BEGGED the youngster to put on her shoes. "Please, honey, put on your shoes. Mommy will buy you something if you'll just do what I ask."

Knowing she had her mother exactly where she wanted her, the little girl asked, "Will you buy me a new puppy?"

"Oh, honey, you know we don't need..."

The girl screamed, "You're mean...You lied...I hate you...I wish you weren't my mother."

The mother sighed. "All right, all right...tomorrow we'll get the dog. Now, put on your shoes and let's sit down and get something to eat. I'm hungry."

How many times have we been disrespectful and not honored someone deserving of it? Worse, how many times have we failed to respect and bring honor to our Heavenly Father—the One Who so rightfully should have our respect?

THOUGHT FOR THE DAY:

Our honor and respect toward others should be evident in our words and deeds. When we respect others, we bring respect to God.

PRAYER FOR THE DAY:

Father, forgive me when I have been disrespectful to You. Help me to always honor You and Your position as my Heavenly Father. My desire is to find what I can do each day to bring more honor to "who You are" and "what You are" to this world.

NOTES:

HANGING IT UP!

"By the rivers of Babylon, there we sat down, yea, we wept, when we remembered Zion. We hanged our harps upon the willows in the midst thereof. For there they that carried us away captive required of us a song; and they that wasted us required of us mirth, saying, Sing us one of the songs of Zion" (Psalms 137:1-3, KJV).

"How shall we sing the Lord's song in a strange land" (Psalms 137:4, KJV)?

When young, I had to pick cotton in order to have money to buy school clothes. It was hard work. The early morning dew would seep into the already scratched hands and it would burn the shallow wounds. On up in the day, I would get thirsty and tired. Hunger pains would rip through my stomach. My cotton sack grew heavy to pull. The strap across my shoulder would tighten with each pound of cotton I placed in the sack. I just wanted to hang it up on the scales, leave the field, never to return.

In Psalms 137 we read there were eight acts of Babylonian captives. They sat down, wept, remembered Zion, hung their harps on the willows, refused to sing a song of the Lord while in captivity, vowed not to forget Jerusalem, prayed for vengeance upon those that rejoiced at their fall, and predicted the fall of Babylon. The captives were in a strange situation, one in which they were very uncomfortable. Maybe they were scared. Perhaps mad at their captors. They might even have been a little apprehensive concerning what might happen in the near future. When they awoke that morning, they certainly didn't suspect to be Babylonian captives. Their world had been turned upside down.

Has your world ever been turned upside down? Has the most unexpected thing happened to you, and you did not know how to handle it? Probably all of us have had episodes in our lives that we would not have chosen. But, how did we handle those times? Did we sit down and weep? Did we "hang our harps" on the willows and say, "I can't sing in this situation?" Maybe, we stopped singing and witnessing about the Lord during this valley in our lives. Did we turn the matter over to the Lord, or did we want to take "things" in our own hands and fix it? Oh, that we might not "hang our harps" up and stop singing even during the bad times.

THOUGHT FOR THE DAY:

Bad times are going to come, but we can make a choice to let them conquer us or we can make up our minds to choose to keep on singing the song of Zion.

PRAYER FOR THE DAY:

Lord, I'm so weak. You are so strong. I pray that during the weakest times of my life that You will replace my frailty with Your strength. I pray that You will remind me of a song I can sing and that I will lift up my voice, even in the dark days, and sing praises to You.

NOTES:

BUT, I WANT TO GO WITH YOU!

"And Naomi said, Turn again, my daughters: why will ye go with me? And they lifted up their voice, and wept again: and Orpah kissed her mother-in-law; but Ruth clave unto her. And Ruth said, Entreat me not to leave thee, or to return from following after thee..." (Ruth 1: 11a, 14, 16a, KJV).

"And Elijah said unto him, Elisha, tarry here, I pray thee; for the Lord hath sent me to Jericho. And he said, As the Lord liveth, and as thy soul liveth, I will not leave thee. So they came to Jericho" (II Kings 2: 4, KJV).

When children are small, they often cry to go somewhere with a parent, a grandparent, or a friend. One can hear the wailing plead, "But I want to go with you." Then the snubbing sets in to add a little more drama to the child's wishes. I can remember not wanting to be left behind when someone was leaving our home. It was so thrilling to hear them say, "Well, all right, come on—you can go." Those words were music to my ears. It never took me long to ready myself for the journey.

In the first chapter of Ruth, we read about Naomi and her daughters-in-law. Naomi, her husband Elimelech, and their two sons, Mahlon and Chilion, had gone to Moab from their home in Bethlehem-judah because there was a famine in their homeland. The two sons met their wives, Ruth and Orpah, and married, settling down in Moab. Later, Elimelech died. Then, a few years later, Mahlon and Chilion died. Being widows, Naomi, Ruth, and Orpah didn't know exactly what their future would hold. Word had come that the Lord had visited His people in giving them bread in Bethlehem-judah, Naomi's homeland. She and her daughters-in-law started on the journey to Judah. Naomi got to thinking about Ruth and Orpah leaving their Moab families behind, so she had a talk with them. Ruth 1: 8 says, "And Naomi said unto her two daughters-in-law, Go return each to her mother's house: the Lord deal kindly with you, as ye have dealt with the dead, and with me." Verse 9 shows us Naomi kissing Orpah and Ruth and they cried. They told her that they would return with her unto her people in Bethlehem-judah. Again, Naomi encouraged them to go back to Moab. They cried some more. Orpah kissed Naomi and returned to Moab. However, Ruth clave to Naomi and wouldn't return with Orpah. Her mother-in-law tried one more time to persuade her to go back with her sister-in-law to their homeland. Then, comes the powerful verse showing Ruth's conviction to go with Naomi. Chapter 1:16 says, "And Ruth said, Entreat me not to leave thee, or to return from following after thee: for whither thou goest, I will go..."

We find another incidence in chapter 2 of II Kings concerning Elijah and Elisha. In verse 2, Elijah told Elisha to stay put—stay behind—because he had to go to Bethel. Elisha wouldn't have it. He said, "As the Lord liveth, and as thy soul liveth, I will not leave thee." So, he got to go with Elijah to Bethel. After they arrived in Bethel, Elijah told Elisha to stay there because he had to go to Jericho. Again, we see in verse 4 where he replied, "As the Lord liveth, and as thy soul liveth, I will not leave thee." So he got to go again. Guess what! Yes, you probably have read down to verse 6 by now where Elijah tells Elisha to stay where he is because the Lord is sending him to Jordan this time. You can guess what Elisha said! Verse 6 shows us Elisha went with Elijah to Jordan. He wanted to go and he did!

Have you ever wondered how the Lord would feel if we were so committed and excited about following and going with Him?

THOUGHT FOR THE DAY:

Following and going with the Lord is my top priority today. I will tell my Father that I want to go every step of the way with Him in my life. Can I truthfully say, "Where He leads, I'll go?"

PRAYER FOR THE DAY:

Father, I am not worthy to go with You through the seconds, minutes and hours of this day, but it is my desire to be with You.

Forgive me when I have not been persistent about walking and talking with You.

NOTES:

EXCUSES...EXCUSES...EXCUSES

"And the king said unto Barzillai, Come thou over with me, and I will feed thee with me in Jerusalem" (II Samuel 19:33, KJV).

"And Barzillai said unto the king, How long have I to live, that I should go up with the king unto Jerusalem? I am this day fourscore years old: and can I discern between good and evil? Can thy servant taste what I eat or what I drink? Can I hear any more the voice of singing men and singing women? Wherefore then should thy servant be yet a burden unto my lord the king? Thy servant will go a little way over Jordan with the king: and why should the king recompense it me with such a reward" (II Samuel 19:34-36, KJV)?

Well, Mr. Barzillai was loaded with excuses! David wanted him to be in his council chamber in Jerusalem because of his wisdom. Barzillai felt he was beyond being able to do the things he knew David would ask of him. So, he started making excuses why he couldn't make the trip. He started his excuses by asking a question about whether he would live long enough to make the journey. He seemed to think it would be too long a trip and he would grow weak. Barzillai told David he had hearing problems and tasting difficulties. He brought up the fact that he was too old and would be a burden to David. Also, Barzillai was concerned that he might not be able to discern between good and evil.

In II Samuel 19:37 we read that Barzillai asked David to let him die in his own city and be buried by the grave of his father and mother. David was bound to have been disappointed that his faithful servant Barzillai declined his invitation. But, the old servant suggested that David take a servant named Chimham, a younger man. David answered in II Samuel 19:38 by saying, "Chimham shall go over with me..."

How many times have we made excuses to God when he asked us to do something for Him? It is so easy to tell the Lord that we would like to do what He is asking, but we just don't see how we can follow through with the plan. The Lord, like David, must be disappointed beyond words at our flimsy excuses we make to Him. How sad when the Lord turns to someone else to do His work because we excused ourselves of doing what He asked.

THOUGHT FOR THE DAY:

How many times has the Lord heard me make excuses to Him? Have I failed to answer, "Yes, Lord, I'll be more than glad to do what You are asking of me?"

PRAYER FOR THE DAY:

Father, in my busy life I pray that You will be my top priority—that nothing will be more important to me than serving You. Please forgive me when I have turned a deaf ear to Your calling, and made an excuse.

NOTES:

ARE YOU BITTER?

"Forbearing one another, and forgiving one another, if any man have a quarrel against any: even as Christ forgave you, so also do ye" (Colossians 3:13, KJV).

"Then Joseph commanded to fill their sacks with corn, and to restore every man's money into his sack, and to give them provision for the way: and thus did he unto them" (Genesis 42: 25, KJV).

What do the two verses above have to do with each other? Well, Joseph's brothers disliked him because their father favored him. All but one brother wanted to kill Joseph. Reuben was against his brothers plotting to take Joseph's life, so he suggested they cast him into a pit in the wilderness. So, the other brothers went along with Reuben and did what he suggested. They stripped Joseph out of his coat of many colors and left him in the pit. Some Midianite merchantmen came along and helped him out of the pit and sold him to the Ishmeelites for twenty pieces of silver, and Joseph was brought into Egypt.

At the time, Egypt's king was Pharaoh. King Pharaoh dreamed some disturbing dreams. It was told him that Joseph could interpret the dreams, so the king sent for him. Because he was able to interpret the dreams, Pharaoh gave Joseph a very important job-—the overseer of the king's house and the land of Egypt. One day Joseph's brothers came to buy corn in Egypt because there was a famine in their land. Joseph was the governor over the land, and it was he that sold to all the people. He recognized his brothers, but they did not know him. But, guess what Joseph did! Forgiveness arrived on the scene of his heart and he commanded to fill their sacks with corn, and gave them provision for the way.

What a powerful story of forgiveness and love! Joseph could have been seriously bitter and nurtured a grudge toward his brothers who had done him wrong. He could have had revenge in his heart toward them. But, instead, he not only escorted bitterness out of his heart, but he rolled out the carpet for grace, mercy, and forgiveness to have front row seat in his life.

THOUGHT FOR THE DAY:

Bitterness will only destroy the person who owns it in their heart. It is debilitating to one's life. Bitterness cripples. Genuine forgiveness is the only way bitterness can be kept at bay.

PRAYER FOR THE DAY:

Father, please help me not to become bitter toward someone. Help me to be able to forgive hurtful actions toward me by another. I pray I will never become a bitter person with revenge in my heart.

NOTES:

PEACE AND QUIET

"And my people shall dwell in a peaceable habitation, and in sure dwellings, and in quiet resting places" (Isaiah 32:18, KJV).

"And they found fat pasture and good, and the land was wide, and quiet, and peaceable..." (I Chronicles 4:40, KJV).

Often when I was a young, my family would take walks in the woods. The many different birds flying overhead and the parade of butterflies in the air fascinated me. Tree leaves whispered sweet soothing sounds in the breeze. Little creeks flowed joyfully in the valleys, and the hills above stood majestically; towering, strong, and powerful. Yet, nothing intrigued me as much as what we called the "Big Rocks" high in the hills. I climbed on top of these huge stones in the middle of the woods, sitting on the highest one to view nature above and below. Never has there been a quieter, more peaceful place than what these big rocks afforded me.

Those days of my youth have since gone and now in my older years I long for a quiet place to sit; a soft mossy pad down by a river or high on a hill overlooking a field of wildflowers.

Even Christ went up in the mountains to get away from the crowd so He could be quiet, peaceful, pray, and think. His desire is that we often be still and think about Him. Jesus doesn't want us to get so busy that we don't take the time to find our quiet place and spend time with Him.

Storms in life will come. Our ship may be tossed to and fro. But, there is a resting place that He provides for those who seek it and desire to take advantage of the quietness it offers. Oh, that we might not overlook the opportunities He sends our way to get away from the hassle of life for a little while.

THOUGHT FOR THE DAY:

I will treat myself to some time in a peaceful place today where I will not be bothered by the demands of my too-busy life. I will soak in the restfulness. I will make time to be still and not be in a hurry.

PRAYER FOR THE DAY:

Father, I beg Your forgiveness for my failure to make time to be still and seek a quiet place. I ask You to show me how to make better use of my time so that I don't overlook the opportunities of peacefulness You give me. Help me not to spend so much time in my busy schedule that I forget that You desire me to take time to notice the peaceful surroundings You have so graciously sent my way.

NOTES:

PRAISE HIM ALL YE LITTLE CHILDREN

"From the rising of the sun unto the going down of the same the Lord's name is to be praised" (Psalm 113:3, KJV).

"To the end that my glory may sing praise to thee, and not be silent. O Lord my God, I will give thanks unto thee for ever" (Psalm 30:12, KJV).

We all have received compliments from time to time, and we appreciate others taking the time to say something encouraging to us. Yet, how often do we become prideful and arrogant because someone "bragged" on us? Probably, we all have let kind remarks "go to our head" to the point that we start thinking too much of ourselves. We must remember that there is only One who is worthy of our praise, and that is the Lord. We fail to give Him the credit He deserves for the things He does with us and through us. We often forget that without Him, we could do nothing. As I Corinthians 15:10 states, "But by the grace of God I am what I am..." How many times have we taken a lofty attitude, completely leaving God out of the picture?

Bro. Mike Ragland of Hayden, Alabama has a wonderful way of accepting compliments from others. When someone tells him that he did a good job, Bro. Mike points to the sky and says, "Well, Lord, they're bragging on You again." Oh, that we might brag on God every chance we get, and give Him the great and mighty praise that He so richly deserves.

"The fear of the Lord is to hate evil: pride, and arrogancy, and the evil way, and the froward mouth, do I hate" (Proverbs 8:13, KJV).

THOUGHT FOR THE DAY:

"Pride goeth before destruction, and an haughty spirit before the fall" (Proverbs 16:18, KJV).

PRAYER FOR THE DAY:

Oh, Father, I pray for Your forgiveness when I've had a haughty spirit. Lord, I know that You are the only One to be praised, but sometimes I fail to send the praise right on to You. Help me each day to remember that I can't do anything without You.

NOTES:

EITHER YOU "IS" OR YOU "AIN'T"

"I know thy works, that thou art neither cold nor hot: I would thou wert cold or hot. So then because thou art lukewarm, and neither cold nor hot, I will spue thee out of my mouth" (Revelation 3:15-16, KJV).

"Doth a fountain send forth at the same place sweet water and bitter" (James 3:11, KJV)?

What makes it so hard for us to make up our minds about something? Why do we sometimes make a decision and then drift away from it? We are double-minded at times and unstable in our thinking. James 1:8 states, "A double-minded man is unstable in all his ways." In other words, a double-minded man is two-faced and has characteristics of being hypocritical. My, my, my! Are we one way at church and another way at home? At work? Are we sweet only when we know someone is watching us?

We sing *Oh How I Love Jesus* but we don't always serve Him like we should. We sing *Wherever He leads, I'll Go*, but we don't even show up at church sometimes, much less go witness where and when He desires. Double-standards seem to be the "going thing" these days. We tell our children not to do something, but they see us doing the same thing. We tell our children they should say their prayers, but they never hear a prayer leave our lips. We tell our children they need to go to church. Yet, we ask the church to send the van by to pick them up and we stay at home instead. Oh, ye double-minded! We are so often just lukewarm—neither hot nor cold.

How long is it going to take for us to make up our minds whether we want to serve the Lord 100 per cent? Will we drift along forever not deciding whether we want to give Him our all? Oh, that we not be living a shady lifestyle. I Kings 18:21 reads, "And Elijah came unto all the people, and said, How long halt ye between two opinions? If the

Lord be God, follow him: but if Baal, then follow him. And the people answered him not a word."

THOUGHT FOR THE DAY:

Today is the day the Lord wants us to make up our minds who we are, what we are to do, and how dedicated we are willing to be in relation to Him.

PRAYER FOR THE DAY:

Lord, forgive me for being a lukewarm Christian at times. Father, I need Your help in showing me how NOT to be a wishy-washy Christian. It is so important to me that I find Your will in my life and gain strength from You so I can be steadfast in everything. Help me not to straddle the fence in my dedication to You.

NOTES:

ALONE IN A CROWD

"Now after the death of Moses the servant of the Lord it came to pass, that the Lord spake unto Joshua the son of Nun, Moses' minister, saying, Moses my servant is dead; now therefore arise, go over this Jordan, thou, and all this people, unto the land which I do give to them, even to the children of Israel" (Joshua 1:1-2, KJV).

"...as I was with Moses, so I will be with thee: I will not fail thee, nor forsake thee" (Joshua 1:5b, KJV).

Have you ever been in a crowd and felt very lonely? Have you had people talking directly to you, but you felt disconnected from them and what they were saying? Do you sometimes feel alone even when your family is near? Have you ever felt that you don't really belong anywhere?

Joshua must have felt lonely for several reasons. His wonderful friend Moses had died. He and the people of Israel probably wondered what they were going to do now that Moses was no longer with them. God had a plan. He had a talk with Joshua and told him that he was to lead the children of Israel unto the land that He had given to them. Can't you just imagine how lonely Joshua must have felt in the middle of all these people who, most likely, were expecting him to do everything exactly the way Moses had previously done? Often leaders live lonely lives even when among a multitude. They want to "fit in" but a leader has to lead, don't they? Can they confide in anyone? Probably not, for fear gossip will start on the rampage. Can a leader "buddy" with individuals in a group? Jealously from others would crucify him; leadership would be damaged.

Joshua knew the children of Israel loved him, but a certain amount of space had to be present between Joshua and the people if he was to be obedient to the Lord and lead the people to the Promised Land. That space just quite possibly may have been lonely for him even in the crowd. Thank goodness, though, in Joshua 1:5b it says,

"...as I was with Moses, so I will be with thee: I will not fail thee, nor forsake thee." Joshua didn't HAVE to feel lonely after hearing those words.

THOUGHT FOR THE DAY:

Lord, when I feel loneliness crowding in on me, I can always know You are there with me. Even when I am in a crowd and feel lonely, You fill my heart and soul with companionship and closeness. Thank You, Father. Thank You.

PRAYER FOR THE DAY:

Father, I pray today for all the people in the world who feel out of place and lonely even in a crowd. Help them to be able to shed this negative feeling with a positive knowledge that You are with them. They don't have to be alone, because You are always near.

NOTES:

YES! YES! WHAT A DAY THAT WILL BE!

"And he arose, and came to his father. But when he was yet a great way off, his father saw him, and had compassion, and ran, and fell on his neck, and kissed him" (Luke 15:20, KJV).

"And Joseph made ready his chariot, and went up to meet Israel his father, to Goshen, and presented himself unto him; and he fell on his neck, and wept on his neck a good while" (Genesis 46:29, KJV).

Not long ago I visited a local nursing home. My husband and I had been asked to sing for the residents that morning. When we arrived, the staff had many of the people sitting in a dining area; some wheelchair occupants, some walking with the aid of walkers, and others moving about with canes. I could not help but notice that a large per cent of the residents sat quietly with a "far away look" in their eyes. Were they like the prodigal son's father (Luke 15) who saw his boy coming home from a great way off? Were they looking for a child to come by to see them that day? Possibly, they were like Jacob—grieving because he thought his son Joseph was dead, until he was reunited with him later. It was very evident that the nursing home residents were looking a great way off trying to see someone or something that meant a great deal to them.

There was an elderly lady who lived close to us. Many times we passed her house when she was sitting on the front porch in her old rocking chair. Yes, she had a "far away look" in her eye, also. Maybe she was seeing in years past when her husband sat on that very porch with her. Possibly, she was looking for someone, anyone, to stop by and visit for "a spell." The little old lady was watching in a front-row seat from her porch.

One of these days we're going to have that "far away look" in our eyes for our Lord and Savior to appear in the sky to take us home with Him. We're going to be watching and waiting for that great reunion day! **Yes! Yes! WHAT A DAY THAT WILL BE!**

THOUGHT FOR THE DAY:

"Watch therefore, for ye know neither the day nor the hour wherein the Son of man cometh" (Matthew 25:13, KJV).

PRAYER FOR THE DAY:

Lord, I pray that Christians everywhere are excited about that great reunion that we'll have with You. May we never stop looking for You and Your return. Father, we ask that we keep that "far away look" in our eyes, anticipating seeing You face to face. **WHAT A DAY THAT WILL BE!**

NOTES:

LIAR, LIAR, PANTS ON FIRE!

"He that speaketh truth sheweth forth righteousness: but a false witness deceit" (Proverbs 12:17, KJV).

"... and he that is unjust in the least is unjust also in much" (Luke 16:10, KJV).

Have you ever lied? Have you ever been TOLD a lie? It's common to hear someone talking about the fact that they only told "a little white" lie. Luke 16:10 shows us that if someone will tell "a little white" lie, they will tell "a big white lie," and think nothing of it. The more one lies, the less they feel guilty. "He that is unjust in the least is unjust also in much." Proverbs 12:17 points out that if one speaks the truth, they show forth righteousness. This same verse reminds us that a false witness brings forth deceit.

I taught school for many years and I heard excuses after excuses concerning students not having their homework. It was obvious that some of the excuses were so absurd that they couldn't possibly be true! Those young students had already gotten into the habit of stretching the truth; their conscience being very sluggish. However, sooner or later the truth had to come out. I often gave "pop test" on the material included in the homework. The grade those students made on the test would tell off on them! Obviously, from their low grade, they had not even looked at the material, much less gotten their homework up on the subject.

If one tells the truth the first time, he or she won't have to remember HOW they told it when they tell it the second time. But, it's sad that some folk tell one lie to prop up another. God knows immediately when we are not speaking the truth. There is no way to fool Him. It's not possible to camouflage the truth with the Lord. He sees right through us, and knows what we're thinking, doing, and saying ahead of time.

THOUGHT FOR THE DAY:

I will ask the Lord to set watch over my mouth; keep the door of my lips, and I will remember that the mouth of a righteous man is a well of life. I will strive to always tell the truth even if I have to suffer for being honest.

PRAYER FOR THE DAY:

"Let the words of my mouth, and the meditation of my heart, be acceptable in thy sight, O Lord, my strength, and my redeemer" (Psalm 19:14, KJV).

NOTES

HELP'S ON THE WAY

"Then Samuel took a stone and set it between Mizpeh and Shen, and called the name of it Ebenezer, saying, Hitherto hath the Lord helped us" (I Samuel 7:12, KJV).

"For the Lord God will help me; therefore shall I not be confounded: therefore have I set my face like a flint..." (Isaiah 50:7, KJV).

In I Samuel 4 we read how Israel was defeated by the Philistines. It tells us that the Philistines put themselves in array against Israel and that Israel was smitten before the Philistines, and they slew of the army in the field about four thousand men. The people of Israel questioned why God had allowed this to happen. If you will read on through Chapter 7, you will see that things changed, however. The children of Israel said to Samuel, "Cease not to cry unto the Lord our God for us, that he will save us out of the hand of the Philistines." Verse 10 shows the Philistines drawing near to battle against Israel again. But, the Lord thundered with a great thunder upon the Philistines that day, and discomfited them and Israel defeated them. Then we come to verse 12. What a comforting, encouraging verse! It tells us that Samuel then took a stone and set it between Mizpeh and Shen, and called the name of it EBENEZER, because there the Lord had HELPED THEM.

Often our lives seem uphill and overwhelming. We feel defeated, worn out, fed up, and stressed to the limit. We don't know what is going to happen next, and if there will be a way to handle it. BUT, praise God from Whom all blessings flow, there's always HELP ON THE WAY! He's ready to intervene on our behalf. We must never cease to cry unto the Lord our God for help. Is he too busy to come to the rescue? Never! Is He tired of hearing our request for help? Absolutely not! Does the Lord want to help? Most definitely!

THOUGHT FOR THE DAY:

James 4:2 "...yet ye have not, because ye ask not." I must stop depending on myself and start depending on God to help me.

PRAYER FOR THE DAY:

Father, there have been so many times when I have fretted because things seemed so helpless and so hopeless. I could have saved myself so much anguish if only I had asked You for help. So, Lord, now I come to Thee asking You to help me seek You in my hours of need, and never cease to pray to You for Your ALMIGHTY HELP.

NOTES:

GOD'S STILL GOOD

"The Lord is good, a strong hold in the day of trouble; and He knoweth them that trust in Him" (Nahum 1:7, KJV).

"O taste and see that the Lord is good: blessed is the man that trusteth in Him" (Psalm. 34:8, KJV).

There is a young couple who attends our church who had a precious daughter named Madison. Oh, how we all loved this little one. She was a picture of health; rosy cheeks, bright eyes, and perfect size. All of us crowded around to get a peek at her the first time her parents, Steve and Katrina McGregor, brought her to church. Shockingly, just a few weeks later, little Madison unexpectedly died. There are no words to describe the grief her parents and other family members felt that day. Her church family cried along with them. Many asked how such a sad thing could happen. Others said nothing; entertaining their own private thoughts. Shortly thereafter when things had calmed down somewhat, this sweet couple returned to church, but without their little Madison. I distinctly remember Katrina walking in with her arms crossed, rather than cuddled around Madison. Her arms were empty, lonely, longing to hold her little one. None of us could feel what this young couple was feeling. No one knew exactly what to say to them. A gloom of grief hung over our very souls. Our pastor, Bro. Jimmy Wilbanks, preached a great sermon that Sunday morning. At the close of the service, Steve McGregor stood and asked could he say something. He walked down the aisle, stepped into the pulpit area, turned to us, and with tears in his eyes said, **"God's still good."** Never had there been such a profound sermon preached in so few words! Needless to say, there was not a dry eye in the church. A calm quietness fell over the congregation and we knew that Steve and Katrina, though devastated, trusted in God to get them through this most difficult time.

Later, during a testimonial service at our church, Katrina stood and proclaimed that if they had not been through this trial, that they would not be the people they are today. PRAISE GOD! GOD'S STILL GOOD!

At Madison's funeral the following poem was read:

MY TINY ROSE BUD

A tiny rose bud from God's garden
was sent to us today.
Her eyes so bright; her skin so soft,
her smile a shining ray.

We hold her tight and watch her sleep
so sweetly does she lay.
We tuck her in her bed at night
a prayer for her we say.

A tiny rose bud from God's garden
my little one so dear.
We'll help you conquer all your goals
and soothe away your fear.

You'll grow to be a lovely rose
to you we'll stay so near.
We'll watch you bloom and grow up strong;
will bring a joyous tear.

Oh, tiny rose bud from God's garden
our plans changed overnight.
The Master willed you to come home
and cuddled you so tight.

We don't know why He took you now
completely from our sight.
But no mistakes He ever makes
the Lord does all things right.

Oh, tiny rose bud from God's garden
our love for you doth grow.
We'll join you in that Heavenly home
the Bible tells us so.

With loving arms we'll hold you close
and never let you go.
Oh, tiny rose bud from God's garden
death isn't the end, we know.

By Martha A. Crawford

****

IN MEMORY OF MADISON MCGREGOR

THOUGHT FOR THE DAY:

Lord, whatever happens to me today, I will trust that You know best. I don't know what tomorrow will bring, but You will take care of it. I can proclaim, **"God's still good."**

PRAYER FOR THE DAY:

Father, forgive me when I question what You do. Please help me to always accept the fact that You know best regardless of what happens in my life. May I always proclaim Your goodness. If YOU do it, it's right. Amen.

NOTES:

TEACHER!

"He taught me also, and said unto me, Let thine heart retain my words...I have taught thee in the way of wisdom; I have led thee in right paths" (Proverbs 4:4a and 11, KJV).

"And he said unto them, He that hath ears to hear, let him hear" (Mark 4:9, KJV).

When I was young my mother would instruct me to be sure and wash my ears when I took a bath. I'm sure she wanted me to be clean, but I'm also certain she wanted to be sure I could ear her when she spoke wisdom to me. The teachings of our parents not only should show us the way in which we need to go, but they should instruct us in how to choose that right way. Our parents should give us good doctrine, teach us how to retain their words in our heart, and give us wisdom and understanding. They should be examples of what they teach us. Even though there are many good teaching parents in this day and time, there are also other parents who don't take the time to teach their children. I noticed the effects of this when I taught school for twenty-five years. It was easy to quickly determine those children who had "teachings" at home and the students who had little or no interaction with their parents. So often, I would tell them to listen to my instructions. Some would. Some wouldn't. I tried to understand my students and put myself in their "shoes," yet still give them guidance I felt they needed regardless of their situations.

WITH MY TEACHER'S EYES

May I see the world through my students' eyes
But still have the wisdom
To change the channel of vision for them
When the call arises;
Sending them on a detour they wouldn't have chosen.

May I see the world through my students' eyes
And, yet, still open up
New avenues for them to take
When they seem to come
To a dead end and have no way out.

May I see the world through my students' eyes
And, yet, not judge
Their sometimes confused views,
But try to add another dimension
To their screen of life that makes colors more vivid.

May I see the world through my students' eyes
And try to understand,
And love,
And guide,
Even when I don't share the same ideas with them.

May I see the world through my students' eyes
And remain encouraging,
Sympathetic,
And Calm,
Rather than dominating, anxious, and unkind about their points of view.

With my teacher's eyes
May I be able to see the world
Through my students' eyes
And still remember
I must show them more than just what's in the textbook.

With my teacher's eyes
May I be able to see the world
Through my students' eyes
As I serve as their
Counselor, confidante, problem solver, and teacher.

By Martha A. Crawford

****

Christ, the greatest teacher of all times, had some who would not listen to His instructions. He knew what they needed to hear. He knew what they were thinking. Yet, some would turn a deaf hear and not heed to His teachings. Christ wanted them to retain His words. He had taught them in the way of wisdom and led them in the right paths. Often, we hear Christ giving us instructions concerning what He wills for us to do. Yet, we don't want to listen. Often, our lives get in a mess when we don't heed His instructions. We whine, complain, and have a pity party because things haven't turned out the way we planned. If only we had paid attention to the GREAT TEACHER'S instructions. If only we had washed our ears out better so we could hear. We so often hear His words, but forget to listen to His instructions. That's when we get our lives in turmoil.

THOUGHT FOR THE DAY:

Today, I will give my full attention to what Christ wants to teach me. I will listen to His voice. He says, "He that hath ears to hear, let him hear" (Matthew 11:15, KJV).

PRAYER FOR THE DAY:

Precious Lord, help me to hear and listen to You. Forgive me when I think I know better than You what I should be doing with my life.

NOTES:

HE KNOWS OUR VERY THOUGHTS

"The Lord knoweth the thoughts of man..." (Psalms 94:11, KJV).

"Search me, O God, and know my heart: try me, and know my thoughts" (Psalms 139:23, KJV).

Often I baby-sit our granddaughter Laney Crawford, daughter of Clint and Tracy Crawford. What a change she makes from week-to-week! She is not talking plain enough for me to understand much of what she says, but I almost always know what she is thinking. Without trying to say anything, Laney will bring me a book, look up at me, and stand waiting on me to sit down with her and read the book. If she gets thirsty, she goes to the refrigerator and points at the door so I'll know she's got juice on her mind. Laney realizes her granny knows what she is thinking. She goes to the glass front door, points in the direction of her swing, and makes a funny little squeal. It only takes a second for her granny or granddaddy to know what she is thinking: outside----in the swing----flying high in the breeze.

You know, the Lord knows what we are thinking all of the time. He doesn't have to ask or ponder to figure out our innermost thoughts. He already knows them. In Matthew 9:1-4 it tells about Jesus pardoning a palsied man. Some standing around watching and listening to Jesus speak to the palsied man said within themselves, "This man blasphemeth." And Jesus, KNOWING THEIR THOUGHTS, asked them why they were thinking evil in their hearts.

Christ knows when we think evil in our hearts. He doesn't have to be told how we feel about anything. He is all knowing and all seeing. Jesus can read our minds. He knows what we are going to think before we even think it. We can keep secrets from each other, but we can't keep anything from Christ.

THOUGHT FOR THE DAY:

How pure are my thoughts? Are the thoughts I think pleasing to Him? Do I remember that Jesus knows what I'm thinking at all times?

PRAYER FOR THE DAY:

Oh, Father forgive me when my thoughts are not pure, clean, and kind. Help me to keep my thoughts pleasing to You. May I always think about You and keep my mind off of things about which I should not be thinking.

NOTES:

LEFTOVERS

"And they did all eat, and were filled: and they took up of the broken meat that was left seven baskets full" (Matthew 15:37, KJV).

"And they did all eat, and were filled: and they took up of the fragments that remained twelve baskets full" (Matthew 14:20, KJV).

When I was growing up, leftovers from one meal to the next were a way of life. It was a survival technique. There wasn't such a thing as throwing anything out after a meal. Each leftover morsel was saved for the next meal; some more being added to it to make a pot-full. Back in those days, it was practically considered a flaw in one's character not to clean their plate, so it was not there that the leftovers were found. They were found in the pots left on the stove. It was always amazing how the woman of the home could make a big meal to feed a husband and eight to ten kids, and still have leftovers. She was skilled at what she did. She looked over the number of family members and knew exactly how many peas to put in the pot and have some left for the next meal.

It reminds me of Christ feeding the four thousand and the five thousand. Matthew 15:37 shows us how Christ looked over the number of people in his presence that day and knew exactly how much food was needed. And, the Scripture tells us there were seven baskets full of leftovers. In Matthew 14:20, there were twelve baskets full of leftovers. Oh, how the Lord knows what we need! The wonderful thing is that He doesn't just give us what we need--- He'll go beyond that and supply us with leftovers.

Jesus not only wants to feed our physical bodies, but He desires to feed our spiritual hunger, also. Are you spiritually hungry today? He has more to offer than you ever dreamed. He'll supply to the point that you'll never hunger or thirst again. There's plenty!

THOUGHT FOR THE DAY:

At times, I have found myself doubting the Lord's ability to meet my needs. But, He has always met my needs and had "leftover" blessings waiting for me. Oh, why can't we trust Him more and more each day?

PRAYER FOR THE DAY:

Father, forgive me when my faith grows weak and I fear my needs won't be met. I often fail to thank You for the bountiful amount of blessings You have sent my way. So many times, I don't thank You enough for supplying not only what I need, but much of what I want. There's always more than enough blessings from You. Thank You!

NOTES:

REMEMBER...FORGET...REMEMBER...FORGET

"And Joseph called the name of the firstborn Manasseh: For God, said he, hath made me forget all my toil..." (Genesis 41:51, KJV).

"Then beware lest thou forget the Lord, which brought thee forth out of the land of Egypt, from the house of bondage" (Deuteronomy 6:12, KJV).

Uh, oh, sometimes I forget to remember to forget. Have you ever done that? Someone hurts our feelings or does some damaging act toward us and we hold it in our hearts and minds and let it "eat" at us. We seem to forget to remember to forget the hurt done unto us. We cling to the mistreatment and nurture it. We have a great pity party. Moving on beyond the hurt doesn't seem to be an option.

In Genesis, we find a man named Joseph who was not treated fairly by Pharaoh. Joseph spent several years in slavery. Later, Joseph was given the position of second in command, took him a wife, and they had two sons. One son's name was Manasseh and the other Ephraim. Genesis 41: 51-52 says, "And Joseph called the name of the firstborn Manasseh: For God, said he, hath made me forget all my toil, and all my father's house. And the name of the second called he Ephraim: For God hath caused me to be fruitful in the land of my affliction." In other words, Joseph chose to remember to forget his hurt and decided to move on and be fruitful for the Lord.

On the other hand, we see in Deuteronomy 6:12 that the children of Israel chose to forget something they should remember, namely what the Lord had done for them. He had taken them through the wilderness forty years and protected them, and given them food. He kept their feet from swelling and kept their clothes from rotting. Yet, they chose to forget to remember His provisions. How could they do such a thing? Well, things got better for them and they didn't give the Lord any credit. They forgot to remember who it was that got them through all of their trials in the wilderness.

So often, we forget to remember the great and wonderful things that the Lord has done for us. But, at other times we don't remember to forget the bad things that humans do to us that cause us pain and anguish.

THOUGHT FOR THE DAY:

I will remember to forget trespasses that come my way today. I will forget the hurt and mistreatment. I will strive to not forget to remember the goods deeds sent my way today—especially those from the Lord.

PRAYER FOR THE DAY:

Father, I want to be like You. In order to do that, I must remember to forget hurtful words and deeds that come my way. I need Your help, Lord, to help me not to forget to remember the great and mighty ways You help me and make my life happy.

NOTES:

MY FRIEND, A VIRTUOUS WOMAN

"Who can find a virtuous woman? For her price is far above rubies" (Proverbs 31:10, KJV).

"Strength and honour are her clothing; and she shall rejoice in time to come" (Proverbs 31:25, KJV).

Frances Louise Moody Simpson was one of the closest friends I ever had. We grew up about two or three miles from each other. Frances and I were like sisters. The two of us played dolls together. We shared our teenage secrets. She and I graduated from high school in the same class. We proudly told each other about our kids and planned to share grandchildren stories, but the Lord took her home earlier than we expected. What a lady she was! Frances was always busy seeing after her husband and children. She loved to sew and would make many of their clothes. Her wonderful cooking kept her family nourished and healthy. My friend's mind was always on her family members. And, she always found time to stretch out her hand to the poor and needy, also.

Strength and honour were her clothing. She had dignity. Frances acted with dignity, dressed with dignity, and treated others with dignity. Verse 26 of Proverbs 31 says, "She openeth her mouth with wisdom; and in her tongue is the law of kindness." Each time my friend and I saw each other, she had a kind word to say to me, and about others.

Proverbs 31:27-28 says, "She looketh well to the ways of her household, and eateth not the bread of idleness. Her children arise up, and call her blessed..." Frances was always busy. She was not lazy. Her days were filled with thoughts of her household. Then, and now, her children call her blessed. Their mother was a virtuous woman. If she were here, however, she would give the honor to God rather than herself. That's what made my friend Frances so special.

THOUGHT FOR THE DAY:

I will strive to make the lives of my loved ones better today. Whatever I have to sacrifice, I will put them first.

PRAYER FOR THE DAY:

Thank You for my family, Father. Help me to always strive to be busy about the things You would have me do to take care of each of them. Most of all, Lord, help them to see You through my words, actions, and deeds. Help me to always act, talk, and think like a lady.

NOTES:

BUTTER, BLOOD, WRATH

"Surely the churning of milk bringeth forth butter, and the wringing of the nose bringeth forth blood: so the forcing of wrath bringeth forth strife" (Proverbs 30:33, KJV).

"He that is slow to wrath is of great understanding: but he that is hasty of spirit exalteth folly" (Proverbs 14:29, KJV).

I remember when I was young that my brothers and I would get in a fuss each time our mother wanted some milk churned. Each one wanted to get to churn first. As far as we were concerned, there were no negotiations. Wrath showed up on the scene. If mother had not intervened, there could have been bloody noses and no butter! But, the wise woman she was, our mother would break off three broom straws. Each straw would be made a different length. She would put them in her hand with one end of the straws hidden. We would draw straws. The one with the shortest straw got to churn first. In the end, there was plenty of butter, no blood, and little wrath.

Proverbs 14:29 reminds us that he has great understanding if slow to wrath. It also says, "But he that is hasty of spirit exalteth folly." In other words, they are short of spirit. They are impatient. It's hard to keep from lashing out at someone who aggravates us. It is also challenging to be patient with difficult people. What we have to remember is that others have to be patient with us. There are times when we provoke friends and loved ones, but we don't want them to say or do anything to get us straightened out! So, by the same token, we must not want to churn their butter, bloody their nose, or bring wrath down on them!

THOUGHT FOR THE DAY:

I will strive to be patient with others today. I want to be gentle and kind toward everyone. It is my desire to treat others as I want to be treated. Today will be the day I will accomplish the great challenge of considering other's feelings before my own.

PRAYER FOR THE DAY:

Thank You for Your patience with me, Father. I know I am not always loving and kind. I praiseYou for the patient folk You have put around me. Please help me remember to be slow to wrath, speak soft words, and treat others the way I want to be treated.

NOTES:

WHO IN THE WORLD SENT OUT THE INVITATIONS?

"He answered and said, Lo, I see four men loose, walking in the midst of the fire, and they have no hurt…"(Daniel 3:25, KJV).

"And he saw them toiling in rowing; for the wind was contrary unto them: and about the fourth watch of the night he cometh unto them, walking upon the sea, and would have passed by them. But when they saw him walking upon the sea, they supposed it had been a spirit…" (Mark 6:48-49, KJV).

Have you ever helped plan a get-together and more showed up than was expected? It occurs to you that the one in charge of sending out the invitations invited more people than you thought. As the guests keep filing through the doorway, you are shocked at the number of people who have suddenly shown up on the scene. Thoughts of despair race through your mind and you wonder if there is enough room for all attending. But, as time progresses not only are you pleased all of the guests came, but you are ecstatic when you realize who some of the guests are in the room with you.

King Nebuchadnezzar ordered Shadrach, Meshach, and Abednego to be put into the fiery furnace. The furnace was exceedingly hot. The flame lapped at the three men with viciousness. They were bound into the midst of the burning fire. After awhile, King Nebuchadnezzar was shocked when he looked into the furnace and saw not three, but four in there. How could that be? There were four loose, walking in the midst of the flames and they were alive and well! Then, it dawned on the king that someone special had been sent to be in the furnace with Shadrach, Meshach, and Abednego. Someone he didn't invite or expect! In Daniel 3:28 it says, "Then Nebuchadnezzar spake, and said, Blessed be the God of Shadrach,

Meshach, and Abednego, who hath sent his angel, and delivered his servants that trusted in him..."

At another gathering, an extra person showed up unexpectedly. We read about it in Mark 6. We find that Jesus had sent His disciples to get into a ship and go to the other side unto Bethsaida while he sent away the people who followed Him. After sending them away, Christ went into a mountain to pray. When evening was come, the disciples on the ship got into high winds and they were toiling in rowing. Guess who showed up!? And, He hadn't even been invited. It was their Lord walking upon the sea telling them, "Be of good cheer: it is I; be not afraid" (Mark 6:50, KJV).

Guests who are not invited sometimes show up and turn out to be the greatest blessing of all those attending. Praise the Lord for the many times He has come to help me when I never thought to invite Him.

THOUGHT FOR THE DAY:

I will remember that my Lord is willing to come into my life, my heart, my soul. All I need to do is send Him an invitation. He'll show up in an instant. The BEST part is, however, that He'll come to my rescue, invited or not, just because He cares.

PRAYER FOR THE DAY:

Thank You for Your divine protection and watch-care over me even when I'm not aware You are hovering around me, Lord. Thank You for showing up even when I didn't send You an invitation. Forgive me for leaving You out of my life so many times. I know Your will is to be with me each day in every event of my world. Thank You.

NOTES:

DAYS OF OUR LIVES

"...we spend our years as a tale that is told" (Psalm 90:9b, KJV).

"To every thing there is a season, and a time to every purpose under the heaven: A time to be born, and a time to die..." (Ecclesiastes 3: 1-2a, KJV).

It is a sobering event to think about how we have lived our lives. Have we been good witnesses for the Lord? Have we been in the Lord's will during our days here on earth? Our lives are like a storybook; beginning, middle, and end. As Psalm 90:9b states, "We spend our years as a tale that is told."

When I was a little girl, my mother would read stories to me and my brothers. We would cuddle up next to her and she would read with just the right emphasis on each word. The story would come alive for us. Often, the tale would begin with, "Once upon a time..." It would often end with, "And they lived happily ever after." A tale about our lives might begin the same way as those told to us when we were young, but it might not end with, "And they lived happily ever after." Sometimes, the tale of our life is displeasing to God because we failed to include Him in it. Oh, how the days of our lives would be better if only He were allowed to mold us into what He wants us to be for Him. Then, and only then, could we say the tale of our life would be one others would want to follow.

From a babe to our elderly years, each season of our life is different. Some of those years are spent growing up, finding our mate, raising children and grandchildren, working, and finding our place in the community. But, the day comes when those things don't demand our full attention. It is in that season of our life that we need to be busier for the Lord than we've ever been. So often, when people get into the "elderly" season of their life, they think they are too old to do anything else for Christ. It is then that they have the prime opportunity to minister to the younger ones around them. What a privilege to teach the children and the younger men and women about life, love, and our Lord. We must live the seasons of our life so that the tale on us will begin and end with, "Once upon a time they lived happily ever after, serving the Lord."

THOUGHT FOR THE DAY:

We reach a point in our lives when we realize we can't be everything to everybody and everywhere all the time. We must make sure, however, that we not let a season of our life pass without working at the most important thing—serving and witnessing for Christ. Then, we can open up the tale about our life, flip through the pages, and say, "I did my best to make a difference for Christ while here on earth."

PRAYER FOR THE DAY:

I know I have messed up so many times during my life, Father. I am so ashamed that the tale of my life has blemishes in it. Please forgive me and help me to go on from this day forward, being careful about how I live, act, and think. My desire is that the rest of the story of my life can be pleasing to You.

NOTES:

THIS IS A HOLD UP!

"And it came to pass, when Moses held up his hand, that Israel prevailed: and when he let down his hand, Amalek prevailed. But Moses' hands were heavy; and they took a stone, and put it under him, and he sat thereon; and Aaron and Hur stayed up his hands, the one on the one side, and the other on the other side; and his hands were steady until the going down of the sun" (Exodus 17:11-12, KJV).

"When Jesus saw him lie, and knew that he had been now a long time in that case, he saith unto him, Wilt thou be made whole? The impotent man answered him, Sir, I have no man, when the water is troubled, to put me into the pool: but while I am coming, another steppeth down before me" (John 5: 6-7, KJV).

Have you ever been desperate for help, but there was none to hold you up—make things easier for you? Why is it in today's world that we don't make the time or the effort to help our fellowman? Is it because we are too busy, self-centered, or non-caring? Or, is it because we simply don't notice the needs of others?

Exodus 17 shows us Amalek and Israel in battle. Joshua did as Moses told him and fought with Amalek. At the same time, Moses, Aaron, and Hur went up to the top of a hill. Verses 11 and 12 tell us that when Moses held up his hand, Israel prevailed, but when he let down his hand, Amalek prevailed. Naturely, after awhile, Moses' arm grew tired from holding up his hand so long, so Aaron and Hur held up Moses' hand. It was a great hold up! God allowed Israel to win! What a blessing to Moses to have two companions who saw his need.

On the other hand, in our verses in John 5, we find quite a different story. Someone had a need, but was overlooked. There was none to hold him up! No one noticed him. I'm talking about the sad man at the Pool of Bethesda who wanted to enter the pool, but couldn't. He had a physical problem, possibly like paralysis, that prevented him from getting into the pool without help so that he could be made whole from whatever disease he had. Jesus saw him and knew he had been there by the pool a long time. Jesus asked, "Wilt thou be made whole?" The poor man told Jesus that when the water was troubled, he wanted to get in but there was none to hold him up so he could enter the pool. And, if that wasn't enough, he told Christ that when it came his turn, someone else would go in before him.

How sad it is when no one holds up another brother in Christ. How awful it is when those in need go unnoticed and are left to themselves. How many elderly are left alone with no one to care? How many children are abandoned each year and have no love? What about the sick who need a ride to the doctor's office? What about the hungry? May we never overlook the opportunity to "hold up someone!"

THOUGHT FOR THE DAY:

I will count it a privilege and an honor to help someone else today. It may interfere with something else I had planned, but I will take the time and opportunity to "hold someone up" today.

PRAYER FOR THE DAY:

Oh, Father, forgive me for all the times I didn't help someone in need. Please forgive me for being selfish and self-centered, thinking I didn't have time to take out of my busy schedule to "hold up" a brother or sister in need.

NOTES:

SHE HATH DONE WHAT SHE COULD

"And Jesus said, Let her alone; why trouble ye her? She hath wrought a good work on me...She hath done what she could..." (Mark 14:6 and 8a, KJV).

"But Martha was cumbered about much serving, and came to him, and said, Lord, dost thou not care that my sister hath left me to serve alone? Bid her therefore that she help me. And Jesus answered and said unto her, Martha, Martha, thou art careful and troubled about many things" (Luke 10:40-41, KJV).

Have you ever done the best you could and someone criticized you? How did you feel? Betrayed? Lonely? Misunderstood? Many times in my life I felt like I was doing something worthwhile, only to find out that others were mocking me, wondering why I attempted to take a certain action.

The above verses portray two different women, but both were being criticized for what they were doing. Mark 14 tells us about a woman with an alabaster box. This box contained precious, expensive ointment. That day Jesus was in Bethany in the house of Simon the leper. The woman having the alabaster box broke the box, and poured this precious ointment on Christ's head. Can't you just hear those around her gasping when she poured this expensive ointment on His head! After all, it could have been sold for a great price. They murmured against her. But, Jesus came to her rescue. He said in verse 6 and 8, "Let her alone; why trouble ye her? she hath wrought a good work on me...she hath done what she could."

We see a similar incidence in Luke 10 concerning two sisters. Mary and Martha had a special visitor at their home—Jesus. Both wanted to do right. Each had a heart for Christ. But, Martha was busy and distracted by things she felt she needed to do to make Jesus feel welcomed. Mary, on the other hand, sat at His feet hanging on every word He said; worshipping Him, and totally in awe of this magnificent guest. Martha grew weary of not having Mary help her, so she complained. In Luke 10:40, we find Martha going to Jesus and saying, "Lord, dost thou not care that my sister hath left me to serve alone? Bid her therefore that she help me." Verse 41 shows us that Christ said, "Martha, Martha, thou art careful and troubled about many things." In other words, He wanted her to leave Mary alone because Mary had chosen the best thing to do—sit at His feet and worship Him. Yes, Martha had done what she could to make Jesus feel welcome, and I'm sure He was appreciative. However, Mary had done even better.

THOUGHT FOR THE DAY:

I will get my priorities in order today concerning what is important in life. I will make sure that I put Christ at the top of the list as THE MOST IMPORTANT. I will not be so anxious like Martha, but will take time to worship Christ like Mary.

PRAYER FOR THE DAY:

Lord, I know I am too busy. I get my priorities so mixed up and You sometimes seen to get pushed to the end of my list. Oh, precious Father, please forgive me for not doing what I can for You.

NOTES:

WAIT! WHERE ARE YOU GOING?

"Nevertheless I have somewhat against thee, because thou hast left thy first love" (Revelation 2:4, KJV).

"...I am the first and the last" (Revelation 1:17, KJV).

How many reading this can remember their first love? Do you remember that first little puppy you got? It was everything you dreamed of as a perfect companion. The little dog followed you, wanted to always be with you, and was happy to see you each day. You loved it beyond all measure. Then, there was that first bicycle. You loved it—a dream come true. Yes, you loved it enough to shine it each day. Oh, and don't forget your first car. Wow! You loved every inch of chrome, every knob, and the radio. But, you never realized what love was all about until you had that first crush on someone. Love had a whole new meaning. You walked around in a daze for days after that first date. Time passed, however, and you went your separate ways. You left that first true love behind, searching for someone or something else to fulfill your life.

The word "left" implies an intentional, rather than accidental, parting. In Revelation 2:4 we read about a church which once was devoted to Christ, but had now lost their eagerness to please and devote themselves to Him. Christ didn't mean what He used to mean to them. Other things got in the way. They had "left" their first love.

In this day and time, we tend to forget that Christ is the first and the last. Our day should start and end with Him. Our devotion should start and end with Him. Our love should start and end with Him. And, of course, our total life should start and end with Him. How often we have "left" Him behind, searching for someone or something that we felt more important. Yet, eventually, emptiness reared its ugly head.

THOUGHT FOR THE DAY:

I will remember that Christ should be my first love. I will think upon Him all day today. I will tell Him how much I love Him and that I can't do without Him.

PRAYER FOR THE DAY:

Even when You keep loving me, Lord, I fail to show You how much I love You. Please forgive me. May I always have a greater love for You than for anything or anyone else. I pray I will let You be the first and last in my life—from birth to death---totally loving You.

NOTES:

OH, HOW HE LOVES YOU AND ME!

"Behold the fowls of the air: for they sow not, neither do they reap, nor gather into barns; yet your heavenly Father feedeth them. Are ye not much better than they" (Matthew 6:26, KJV)?

"Are not two sparrows sold for a farthing? And one of them shall not fall on the ground without your Father...Fear ye not therefore, ye are of more value than many sparrows" (Matthew 10:29 and 31, KJV).

I heard a preacher say at a funeral, "For every sparrow that falls, God attends the funeral." He was using these words to comfort the family. The minister wanted the wife and children of the deceased to realize that God is looking down from Heaven and He understands their pain, loneliness, and grief. God was right there with them.

God made the sparrow. He designed the bird's wings, gave the feathers color, and made it to fly on earth. Yet, not even all of those detailed creations compare to the creation of man. His love for the sparrow can never compare to the love He has for us. Matthew 10:29 says, "Fear ye not therefore, ye are of more value than many sparrows." Did you notice the wording of this verse? It says we are of more value than **MANY** sparrows—not just one of these little birds. It is hard to imagine being loved that much by our Lord. How could He love sinners? We don't know the answer to that question, but we have proof in the Scriptures that He loves us more than anything He created. "For God so loved the world, that he gave his only begotten Son, that whosoever believeth in him should not perish, but have everlasting life" (John 3:16, KJV).

Often, we forget that our God attends to the minutest details. We are so important to Him that He knows how many hairs are on our head! It would take us hours to count all of those hairs, but He already knows the number! He is our Creator. He values our existence. God knows us better than anyone, and He **STILL** loves us.

THOUGHT FOR THE DAY:

He loves me! He loves me! I just can't imagine how He could love a sinner like me.

PRAYER FOR THE DAY:

Father, I can never be worthy of Your unconditional love, but I thank You for caring for me. Help me to show Your love to someone else today.

NOTES:

GRIEVE NOT...QUENCH NOT

"And grieve not the holy Spirit of God..." (Ephesians 4:30, KJV).

"Quench not the Spirit" (1 Thessalonians 5:19, KJV).

Have we grieved or quenched the Spirit? How many times have we given in to wrong tempers, unholy words, or unrighteous action? The Holy Spirit is represented as a fire—to purge, purify, and refine the soul. We give way to sin and grieve the Holy Spirit. The Holy Spirit is the Spirit of love, so anger, malice, revenge, or any unkind or unholy act will quench it so that it will withdraw its influences; the heart being left in a state of darkness. Loving the world and its earthly materialism will grieve and quench the Spirit as much as any ordinary act of transgression.

The Holy Spirit in the soul of a believer should be the means in which we testify that we are God's property, and we should be busy about serving God. If we do not have the Spirit of Christ, then we are none of His own.

We read in Isaiah 63:10, "But they rebelled, and vexed his holy Spirit: therefore he was turned to be their enemy, and he fought against them." The Lord showed favor to Israel and called them His people. He was their Savior. In His love, He redeemed them. Yet, they rebelled and vexed (grieved) His Holy Sprit.

How many times has the Lord allowed and willed us to go to church, but we go there with a bad spirit and attitude? After He had seen fit to allow us to have the good health and the means to get there, we still hung on to our bad thoughts. Was it possible that we quenched and grieved the Holy Spirit that day? Most definitely! Could we have caused the "feeling" in the church service that day to wax cold? Absolutely! Oh, how we must guard against letting unrighteous actions, words, and attitudes quench and grieve the Holy Spirit.

THOUGHT FOR THE DAY:

I will take heed that I don't grieve the Spirit of our Lord today. I will not let temper, bad words, unrighteous actions, and unloving attitudes manifest themselves in my life. I will keep my guard up against quenching the Holy Spirit.

PRAYER FOR THE DAY:

Father, forgive me when I have harbored wrong words, thoughts, actions, and unholy hardness in my heart. I pray that I will never be one to quench and grieve the Holy Spirit.

NOTES:

Printed in the United States
45570LVS00005B/160-168

9 781596 820579